Acknowledgement

My story of "The Stolen Humanity" is dedicated to my children who endured adversity which was not of their own blame.

I am also extending my indebtedness to my extended family, friends, co-workers and especially for my children's love and caring that has overarched my existence.

Above all and to the greatest extent, I honor all mighty God the Yahuwah who kept us refuge in his arms of love.

About the Author

Un Chu Lee-Hoyle is a mental health clinician at the Adult Behavioral Learning Center of Lahey Health Behavioral Services. She has devoted 19 years of her life in the mental health field and began at Health and Education Services in 1999. Her career began as residential worker while studying for her GED at age 52. She then was scouted from a relapse prevention program to work with substance abused individuals and families with court involvement. Later she was promoted to program director of the residential program for patients from State hospitals who are challenged with severe mental illness. She also served two terms as president of Intercultural Family Mission of Boston region as volunteer work. This mission group is a non-profit organization serves underprivileged Korean women in U.S. and mixed race

children who are left behind in South Korea.

Ms. Lee-Hoyle immigrated to U.S. when she was 28 years old with a 6th grade education. She struggled through 2 failed marriages and found herself left alone with 3 children with no extended family to rely on. She worked for a variety of minimum wage jobs, lived in subsidized housing and she was the sole provider for her children.

After 12 years of study, while holding a full-time job with English as her second language, she received her Master's in Expressive Therapy from Lesley University at age 64. When she received her Master's degree, her position was advanced to an individual therapist at an outpatient clinic. She also worked as an In-home therapist for children with DCF (Department of Children and Family) involvement and their families. At age 70, she suffered a heart attack which left her with a damaged heart and an impairing liver condition. Nevertheless, after recovering from her medical condition, she returned to work as part time day treatment clinician. She renders diagnostic evaluations, creates and follows up treatment plans for each student/client. She also generates follow ups with their insurance authorizations to attend the day treatment.

She is surround by her loving family, friends, wonderful co-workers and individuals she serves in the field of mental health.

.

The Stolen Humanity

Awakening from the silent, unutterable state of solitude, it has recourse me to recoil the power of my voice that lies within me. No one can compass the reason why life deals more stringently with some than others. We live in a society where fortune favors the strong and in the same vein, chance only favors the prepared mind. Wherefore, rebuilding shattered life through the muddy landscape is only possible, if I am willing to navigate challenges and paves the way with honesty and ability to withstand.

It also made me realize that my past does not dictate my future and achieving life 'success' can only reaps from the seeds I have sown. When I was young, I let others have power over me, my mind became confused, and unhealthy chronic relationships began to develop. As my sub-consciousness gets feebler, the one holds the power prostrated their territory and I was unwittingly matted in entrapment. I lost the sense of my self-worth and stayed in silence for over six decades. Yet, I survived through many traumatic events because I developed an innate dissociative capacity to breath, dream and live as sound individual.

Still, I lugged an image of a little girl with the unkempt hair, gray sweater, shaggy skirt wearing an old pair of shoes standing far away in misty haze. She is cold, empty and without a voice. Hence at last, near the final phase of my life I am able to embrace her through consolation. "You are safe now, we are safe"...........

Korean National flower

Roses of Sharon

Chapter One

I was born in 1947 in a village called Oak Cheon, in the state of Choong Chung Bookdo in South Korea. Not long after my birth, my parents decided to move their family to a small village called Docjangy. The village they moved to was tucked away in the outskirts of port city Inchon, about 40 miles from the capital city Seoul. My parents named me Un Joo; the spelling of Un was taken from my father's first name Un Moung. At the time it was unusual for girls to be named after her father because girls were not counted worthy. My parents had 6 children before me- they lost 3 of them to mysterious death, all before they reached their second birthday. The children who died were born after my older sister, and now my mother conceived her 7th child, which was me.

My mother was frantic and determined to save the 7th child and sought help from the local medium. The medium told her to take the first spelling of father's name, supposedly to prevent the early death (Thus how I got my name Un Joo). Un means 'silver' and Joo means 'wonderer' or a 'traveler'. When I left Korea in 1976, the American embassy misprinted the spelling and I've been called Un Chu ever since. Sometimes people pronounce "Woocha" or "Achoo" and another said "God bless you". I thought about legally correcting the spelling, but then I'd have to change everything from social security to citizenship, driver's license and so-on and I decided to leave as is.

My mother never talked about the reason why my older sister was sent to live with our maternal grandmother, but she returned home when I was 3 years old. My sister and mother did not get along very well and my sister spread the rumor in the neighbor that she was adopted. I think I can understand her resentment towards our mother, because if I was sent away from my home to live with the grandmother, I would probably feel the same way. The Docjangy is a small village that settled on the hillside of the lower mountain, where a population of less than few thousand consisted of mostly farmers and fishermen. Mother told us that on weekends there was an open market in town square where people sold home grown vegetables, fresh caught fishes, seasonal fruits and multi grains. There would be stands with sweet treats where the kids would gather around with twinkling eyes. She said that the best treat in the summer was a slush stand, with man who spins the wheel that is attached to the ice box and crush ice into slushes. He would spray color on top of crushed ice while kids watch in awe, mesmerized.

Not many people know about Korean history other than Korean War, but the ancient Korea existed from 10.000 BCE or even earlier by people who subsisted on hunting, fishing and gathering. Korea is a small country known as the 'Land of morning calm' where people strive for contentment with moral courage and integrity. Our national flower is 'Roses of Sharon' and the fertile soils are rich in steels and metals throughout Northern land. The first record of the roses of Sharon grown in Korea is mentioned in an article produced 1, 400 years ago. It stated in mythological fiction, Xuanzhongji in Chinese writing that written in the Eastern Jin Dynasty of China, mentioned "The Land of Wise-men is spread for 1,000 miles where mugungwha (roses of Sharon) flowers bloom plentifully (history of national flower of Korea). This fertile land was an envy of surrounding countries especially to the Japanese and long-standing conflicts existed between two countries for centuries.

Sadly, as stated by Korean history, one of the Japanese invasions was in 1592 which lasted until 1598. Then, in the early hours of October 8,1895 a group of

Japanese military rushed deep into the Korean royal chamber and dragged out the Queen. They stabbed her multiple times, stripped her stark naked, sodomized, and raped her. Then, while the Queen was still alive, she was doused with kerosene and set on fire and they watched her burn. The history indicated that she was previously advised to change her identity by wearing one of the female officers "Sanggooung" attire in order to avoid the harm coming to her. Regardless of that advice, she refused to disguise her identity as queen and set firmly on her throne. She also fully dressed in empress's costume to face the Japanese militaries with the dignity. The history also indicated that she never once showed fear, even to the point that while she was being stabbed, stood in masquerade sternness and calmness as the queen of her nation. She was the last empress of Korea called Myeongseoqng, who spearheaded are-organization and modernization of Korea's military. She also reached out to China, Russia, and the other western powers to play them off against the Japanese in hopes of protect Korean sovereignty. The Japanese history indicates she perished that same day. However, the Russian personnel who witnessed the crime stated someone put

out the fire and she lived for 3 days with the ghastly pain before she took her last breath. (from History) Korean

the However, who Russian personnel witnessed

13

the crime stated someone put out the fire and she lived for 3 days with the ghastly pain before she took her last breath. (from Korean History) The last empress's love for her country, permanency continues to resonate through the modern day of Korea.

The reason I am focused on the history of Korea in my memoir is because I want readers to understand who I am as Korean and our rich histories that many people do not know. Many people picture Korea as "MASH", the TV show that aired in 1970 and the Korean war in 1950. I've always known our nation's history because it was passed down from generations, and we studied in elementary school. In consideration of the pursuit of my autobiography, I took a considerable amount of time to research and find far more historical information about my country, and it needs to be shared. I am now more so richly knowledge with my own ancestors and exhilarated by their steadfastness and the vigorous convictions. I also feel that it is important for readers to know about my ancestry, because knowing where and who I came from gave me the courage and certitude to tell the truth, the audacity to reclaim my rights as an individual, as human being and to claim the power of my voice that existed in me.

In 1910 the Korean Empire was once again annexed by the empire of Japan after years of war. The Korean independence was severed in order to establish control, the empire of Japan waged an all-out war on Korean culture. The Korean peninsula was ruled by Japan and Koreans were not allowed to speak, sing or write with their own language, and all individual names were changed to Japanese names. They exploited our people in our own land with marginalization of our history and culture. The environmental exploitation of the Korean peninsula lasted for 35 years. There were some 200.000 young Korean girls who were forced to the war front, to serve the Japanese army as sex slaves until the end of the World War II.

Many girls died from physical and sexual torture along with the starvation and suffering from disease before the war was over. When Korea regained independence in 1945 only 7.000 sex slaves were set free and returned to the homeland in Korea. I was familiar with the story because I visited Korea around 2008 and had the chance to participate in protests with the Mission group I was involved in. We were in front of the Japanese embassy in Seoul Korea, with thousands of other protesters including the survivors who were forced into sexual slavery for imperial Japan during World War II. We ask their government to acknowledge their crime against these women and yield apology, but they kept silent.

In spring of 2015, I had the privilege to meet one of the survivors of "comfort women" with close members from Non-profit organization while protesting in front of Harvard Kennedy school in Cambridge, MA. At that time the Japanese Prime Minster Abe Shinzo was scheduled to give speech at Kennedy school. Many Koreans from surrounding areas were gathered to protest once again, to ask for acknowledgement of their wrong doing and an official apology for women who were victimized. Abe Shinzo kept his silence and refused to show his face. He entered the Kennedy school through the back door while a team of Japanese security personnel protected him from public view. Just as some people refused to believe that the Holocaust never existed, the Japanese government refuses to admit their force of Korean women to sex slavery, they called "Comfort Women". The day before the protest, me and my colleagues from an organization (I was serving second term as the president of Massachusetts region) had time to set with Ms. Yi and hear from her own experiences.

Ms.Yi was one of the survivors from Japanese sex slavery during World War II who was brave enough to speak out after 70+years of being in silence. We all gathered around Ms. Yi and listened to her most horrifying and heart wrenching stories  about the thousands of girls who were captive in Japan. Many of them were in their early teens from age 13 and on. She remembered how they were sodomized and tortured inside ships on their way to Japan or China, wherever the Japanese militaries occupied. Ms. Yi said that those young girls, including herself, were raped by Japanese soldiers, ratio of one girl to 100's of men. She said that the 1/3 of the girls died from torture and were thrown off the

18

ships to the ocean. Ms. Yi is among a few dozen survivors who are still living, traveling all over Korea and the US to give testimony from their own experiences. I believe she was in her early 90's when I met her. She was kidnapped from her village by Japanese soldiers. She said that some girls were coerced for factory work or for housekeeping jobs. Even after the war was over the Japanese military brothels, which they called "comfort stations" continued to operate in Japan and refused to release the girls. When the girls finally returned home, there was no 'welcome home' tributes; rather they became societal outcasts from their own people and even from their own families. Ms.Yi told the Washington Post in 2015, "I don't want to hate or hold grudge, but I can never forgive what happened to me." She also stated in our meeting, " I am so disgusted for being called comfort women, because I never wanted to give comfort to those men", "I just want their apology". One by one, these women will be gone and no one left to tell the story and soon we'll all be forgotten. Some said "The past in the past and just let it go". Though, our country has come a long way from the past, but the ugly truth cannot be erased. I understand all about "forgiveness" and we may not need to hate each other, but the history will "repeat" if we don't take heed for what happened.

My mother often shared stories about her life during the Japanese rule in our country. She remembers having to give up their rights as Koreans, including language, singing, writing and had to be called by Japanese names. During their occupation, Japan took over Korea's labor and land. Nearly 100.000 Japanese families settled in Korea with the free land they had been given by Japanese government, and nearly 725.000 Korean workers were made to do forced labor in Japan. My mother's parents lost all their wealth to Japan, and she remembers selling eggs on the street to help support her family, and my father was forced to service in the Japanese military.

She said that she could not speak Japanese well and she mis-pronounced egg (which was 'tamago'), but instead she yelled out 'omanko' which means 'intercourse'. A Japanese man rushed out from his house, swung a sword and swore at her saying "chikushou baka yarou, watashi wa subete no anata korosudesho!!" which it meant "you damn idiots, I will kill all of you!". My mother was so scared, she dropped the egg basket and ran for her life. The Japanese also built the shrines using Korean laborers and Korean government funds to build their own Shinto Shrines and it became a place of forced worship. The Japanese government made Koreans to "worship the gods of imperial Japan, including dead emperors and the spirits of war heroes who had helped them conquer Korea earlier in the sentry." (by historian Donald N. Clark) My mother said that if anyone attempted to disobey their rules, he/she would be jailed or beheaded in the public square in order to set an example for others. She witnessed Korean women, men and children who were infected with the stomach virus, were shoved into holes in the ground they dug, sprayed with gasoline and set on fire. Those images haunted my mother frequently throughout her life.

My mother was born into wealthy parents; in fact, her father held third highest governing body in king's palace and they possessed most of the land in the village where they lived. She said in such a way, once her father entered the palace to conduct the executive regime with the king and other governors, he would remain there for weeks at a time. There would be entourages with horsemen and a carriage that my grandfather would sit in tall and parade through the streets to his home. She was the only child to my grandparents and the heir of all their wealth. Growing up she had the privilege to have personal attendants who followed her around to aid her needs, whatever that might be. Her parents had many servants from cooks to gardeners, personal attendants and so on. My mother said that when she was in her teens, she fell in love with one of the servant boys, which was forbidden for her family tradition. Of course, her parents never knew what was going on with their daughter and her father has chosen a young man from the line of Yi dynasty as her future husband. My maternal grandfather believed that the Yi dynasty would rise again when the time was right and when they did, his son-in-law would be sure to rise with the power. Thus, my grandfather took him in to their home and allowed him to stay in separate quarter where he studied and slept until he married my mother.

My father who is the line of Yi dynasty, was a tall, handsome young man with thick wavy hair, straight nose with big brown eyes and a beautiful set of straight white teeth. He was sophisticated, taught and poised as a person of royalty. Nonetheless, he was forced to serve in the Japanese military just like everyone else when Japanese ruled the Korea. My mother was a petite and pretty young woman who was born with the "silver spoon" in her mouth and would not know the meaning of "sorrow" if it wasn't for the Japanese invasion of Korea. I don't think either of my parents loved each other but they embraced marriage and had total of 10 children. It was not unusual for parents to arrange marriage for their children in those days. Women are taught to be submissive to their man and eventually they love and respect the one whom they call 'husband'. Luckily, I was born 2 years after Korea gained independence from Japanese rule in 1945. Sadly, during the occupation in Korea, my maternal grandfather was kidnapped by the Japanese government and all his fortune disappeared with him; he was never to be seen again.

Now I need to further explain the fragment of Korean history because it is related to my family tree. Korea was originated from Dan-Gun which means the tribe of 'Dan', traveled from somewhere in middle east Asia through Turkey, India, Mongolia, China and ended up in a small land of Asia and established the nation "Dan" followed by "Joseon" than "Yi Dynasty" and later named Korea. Through my research, I believe that our nation traveled even further from Syria where they started embedding the Roses of Sharon as their nation's flower, carried and replanted wherever they migrated. I remember when I was coming to America, I saw an old Korean man who had a carry-on bag that has small "Roses of Sharon" sticking out of it. It is known for many Koreans to plant our national flower wherever they call "home". In fact, I planted one in front of my last ex-husband's house, which has now grown over 10 feet tall. Prior to becoming Japan's captive, Korea was called Joseon or Yi Dynasty. Joseon dynasty was the Korean Sovereign State founded by the King 'Taejong' who is my ancestor, and the dynasty lasted

from 1392-1897, approximately five centuries. The king 'Sejong the Great' who created the Korean writing and was loved by his people was the third son of King Taejoug. King Taejong had four sons, but the first-born prince denounced his kingship. He was known to love to drink rice wine and spent most of his life as a wandering poet. The second prince, who is the direct blood line of my lineage, also was not interested in politics. He chose to become a Buddhist monk, build several temples, surrounded himself in solitude and led a humble life. He expressed humility by serving people who were in need. He never denied his king/brother's request for his advice and always welcomed him when the king needed tranquility and rest from the burden of being a king. I was so thrilled to find the original portrayal of him in online historical sites as well as the photo of him and his wife's cemetery. I am also ecstatic and enchanted by the modern day's Yi Dynasty, and the line of my ancestors still gather annually to commemorate his life once lived. They even have a song about my direct ancestor as the great humanitarian who divulged his warranted kingship to his brother so his country would prosper. As I am writing this, I heard the song for the very first time, which pierced my heart and longed for renaissance of my own existence.

The Joseon-Yi dynasty was the last royal heritage and later became the imperial dynasty of Korean history. It was the longest ruling Confucian dynasty in Korean history. The image of King Sejong (my great, great...uncle) and his work continued to be honored by Korean people to this day and his portrait is printed on 10.000 won (Korean currency). His statue was erected at the center of Gwanghaw gate square in Seoul in 2009 to honor his work. The statue stands 9.5-meter high, with bronze on top of the concrete pedestal and continues to be honored and admired by many. Following the surrender of Japan in 1945, American administrators divided the peninsula along the 38th parallel, with United States troops occupying the

southern part and the Soviet troops occupying the northern part of Korea. The failure to hold free elections throughout the Korean peninsula in 1948 deepened the division between the two sides, and the North established a communist government by dictator Kim ill song, (grandfather of current dictator Kim Jong Un) aided by the Soviet Union.

In the early morning on Sunday June 25, 1950 the alarming sound of bombs broke the silence of the dawn and the first significant armed conflict of the Cold War had begun; I was 3 and half years old. Although, the war only lasted for three years, it did much damage and inflicted pain upon many lives, including my own. Homes were burned, families were divided, people were injured, or killed and our nation was left with vagabonds and orphans wandering the streets.

People were suffering from physical, psychological and emotional traumas. My parents first born son, my oldest brother Teck Joo, was captured by North Korean soldiers and taken hostage by gunpoint when they were fleeing to the north peninsula when the war was ending. My parent's second child died during the war by drowning. Their fourth, fifth and the sixth child died of unknown causes, all before they reached their second birthdays. My older sister, who was the third child, was sent away to our maternal grandmother before I was born and returned home when the war broke out. She was thirteen years old when she came home. My sister soon became my caretaker when we had to flee further down south to escape from the North Korean military.

I don't have a lot of memory about the war but I have bits and pieces of vivid

memories about what we would eat and the places we stopped for lodging when the night fell. My sister said that we had to walk miles, sometimes in the rain, and saw many dead bodies scattered all over the streets. She described wanting to walk with her eyes closed so she didn't have to look at the dead bodies, but then I would step on them. She added "you are so lucky that you don't remember those things because you probably die from having too many nightmares". However, I do remember vacant barns and shacks usually filled with refugees trying to get some shut eyes before the long journey ahead of them. I also remember seeing people slaughter poor cows that were left behind, and they'd boiled the cow in a large pot over the fire. People, young and old would gather around the pot and slice meat with the butcher knife or bite pieces off like animals. Those horrible images kept me from eating any meat until I was in my 20's.

Our maternal grandmother was a noble woman with strong will. She was

born in south province call Gyeogsang
Bukdo, known for people with the strong
personality but also known as the people
of honesty and loyal to their family and
friends. She lost her husband and all their
wealth to Japanese government and she
became a commoner, but she held her
head up high and showed no weakness.
She refused to flee from North Korean
soldiers and asked us to go without her,
because "no one will drive me out of my
own home even if death comes to me".
Knowing her stubbornness, my mother
wept as we set out to journey without her
to our unknown destination. I am not
exactly sure how many days or weeks we
were into the journey but, my mother
could not baring the thought of her
mother who may face harm from North
Koreans. At last she convinced my father
for us to return home to check on her
mother. When we arrived at the Incheon
late at night, the whole city was scorched
by fire; but miraculously, my
grandmother was alive. After returning to
the city, we were living in constant fear;
Nevertheless, in July 1953 the war finally
ended. The General Macarthur landed on

the port of Inchon with his troops to save the city from the North Korean military. The news quickly spread throughout the villages and the North Korean soldiers took many hostages to cross over the 38th parallel.

Among those hostages was my oldest brother Teck Joo who, in his late teens was also taken at gun points with other teens from the city. I was 6 ½ years old when he was taken away from us. My brother Teck Joo was handsome just liked my father. He was kind and always looked after me and I loved following him around whenever he let me. He often carried me on his back and tried to make sure that I was fed and safe, and I missed him terribly when he was gone.

Life after the war was harsh for many people in South Korea. The families were separated, famine and disease quickly spread throughout the country. People were suffering from injuries, dying from starvation and diseases. There were orphans and vagabonds roaming the streets, knocking on every door begging for food. There were many American military bases in South Korea after the war ended, including the base in our hometown which later vacated. Once a week, people lined up behind the military base and waited for table scraps to be brought out from the GI cafeteria. The "house boys" who worked in the "chow hall" inside the base would bring out the huge drums of scraps from plates and sell them for small changes. Sometimes we would find pieces of meat, or soggy bread floating on the slurry water and sometimes cigarette butts. I remember standing in line with the large coffee can that I found in the dumpster with tightly held change in my palm. As I wiped sweat from my forehead, I anxiously waited, hoping that scraps wouldn't run out before my turn came. When I finally reached behind the truck, the house boy would fill the can with the sour smelling residue. Sometimes it splashed and hit my face or my clothes, but I didn't care as long as my empty can was filled. I would then hurry home, and my mother would carefully pour my can into the pot and add few tablets of saccharine to boil over the little stove before eating them. My father would not dare to eat it because he was too proud.

One winter evening, an unknown young soldier visited our home with a large brown box. Inside the box, we found colorful, shiny hard candies and a beautiful bluish green coat with a matching pair of mittens that fit me perfectly. I thought they were the most beautiful things I had ever seen in my life and I wore them almost every day until the spring came. I could still remember the soldier's face. He had blue eyes and white skin with freckles on his face and when he smiled, one side of his cheek mounds. I did not understand then, but now I am thinking, he was probably chowing tobacco. If I close my eyes, I could almost see the greenish blue color and the scent of the coat still fresh in my mind....

In our village there was a girl who was the same age as I was and she always looked pretty. She wore floral printed dresses and a ribbon wrapped around her pony tail and most of all she wore beautiful white sandals to school in summer. Most of the girls in our village, including me, wore rubber shoes and if you are lucky enough, maybe you would have pair of sneakers for special occasions. Oh, how I wished that I could have a pair of those white sandals. One day my father let me keep the change from getting cigarette for him, and bought a sheet of white construction paper. I waited until everyone in my family fell asleep, and then I quietly set in the corner of the room and designed my own sandals with the construction paper using needle and thread. I carefully wore them to outside and beneath the faint street light

it almost looked as real sandal and I
pranced around like the princess.

Chapter Two

My parents never got over losing their
first-born son to North Koreans. I often
heard my mother's ill fainted cries in the
dark. She would kneel down on the dirt
ground in the back yard with the small
table in front of her. She would fill the
bowl of freshly drawn water from the
well and pray and beg to God in heaven to
bring her son back home. She would
prepare a special meal on his birthday
and kept the rice bowl warm so he would
be fed, if he walked through the door...
but he never came home. Eventually, she
fell into a deep depression and my father
sought alcohol to numb his emotional
pain. Nonetheless, they managed to have
three more children, one boy and two
girls; but no other child mended their
broken hearts from losing their firstborn
son. Their lack of parenting angered my
older sister, and her resentment toward

37

my parents often was evident when she lashed out on me. When our parents were not around, she'd beat me, pull my hair, stripped clothes off from me and lock me in the room naked. She'd yell out "you such a stupid girl, it's all your fault, see what you made me do?" "I wish you were never born at all, then I don't have to deal with your nonsense". If I cry, she'd said that I looked even uglier, with a wrinkly face like an old woman. I was known as a "clumsy" child, because of bruises scratches or having bloody noses. One time she hit my head so hard with the metal scooper, it was cut open and bled heavily. She then threatened me, that if I ever told our parents about what happened, she'd kill me and bury me somewhere that no one could find. Sadly, my sister wasn't the only one whom I had to battle with physically and emotionally. My mother often hit me with a bamboo stick when she was frustrated and my father used to kick me or throw me across the room when he was drunk.

One day my father was playing with my little brother on his lap and I tried to sit with him. My father then kicked me I landed on top of the dirty diapers in the corner of the room. My face plunged into the poppy diapers but I didn't get up because I was too embarrassed for being rejected. My father was known a 'wise' and 'noble' man, who would give the shirt off his back if someone needed. He had many friends and neighbors who respected him, because he was known to be a kind, gentle and giving person. Please, don't get me wrong, I do have some fine memories of my father when he was sober. Once he took me and my younger brother fishing at the little creek miles away from our home. We packed our lunch in our knapsacks, rode the bus, then walked beside the rice paddy to the creek. We had fun catching grass hoppers, eating away grains on rice stalks and enjoy in g the warmth of a sunny afternoon. We caught small fishes from the creek with an insect catcher we made out of a net and stick. The water on the creek was cool and so clear that we could see smooth pebbles beneath the stream while fishes hurried from one stream to another.

Once when I was about 7 years old, I fell into a small pond near our home and I nearly drowned. Fortunately, one of our neighbors walked by and saw me bobbing from the pond and pulled me out of the water and called for help. When my father came to the scene, he beat the crap out of me for being 'stupid'. I never learned how to swim because my mother warned me never to go in deep water. She said that the fortune teller told her I had a greater chance to die by drowning, just like one of my older brothers who drowned during the Korean war. Even to this day, I am scared of water deeper than 3 feet. The only place I feel safe in the water is the bathtub. There is one more thing I want to share, that you may have a hard time believing. Not long after the pond incident, my mother went to visit her mother who lived alone. My mother visits her from time to time to make sure she is doing okay. That day I stayed home with my sister and our younger brother. I don't remember what triggered my sister's anger but she took off all my clothes and locked me in the room naked. When I heard laughter of neighborhood kids who were playing outside and I was curious.

I found some clothes from the pile of laundry and put them on, lifted the latch on the door and walked out, only to get caught by my sister. She dragged me by my hair and tried to shoved me back to the room. Before she had chance to shut the door, I pushed through the door and started to run; she ran after me. I got my feet up fell to the ground; moments later she caught up with me. With our brother on her back, she stomped her foot on my neck, and I screamed, which made our brother cry. She got distracted by his crying and I got up and ran until I was out of her sight. I was then too afraid to go back home because I believed my sister would kill me. So, I walked and walked. I passed the city lines, farms, rice paddies and found myself on the mountain side with the sun beginning to set. I suddenly realized I didn't know where I was and I couldn't find my way back home even if I wanted to. I kept on walking until I came to the hillside of the mountain. I was tired, hungry and scared. I sat on the grass, head down between my knees and cried again, not knowing what to do. Suddenly, I raised up my head I saw village far from where I was sitting.

I got up and start to run fast as I could. As I was getting closer to the village, I saw smoke coming up from the chimney of someone's house. I thought to myself, "Someone must to be cooking dinner". Then I saw woman with the black and white Korean outfit churning something in the wooden churner. My eyes got widened and I gasped- it was my mom!! It was my grandmother's house!! Can you imagine how thrilled I was? My mom was startled and flabbergasted "what on earth are you doing here all by yourself, crazy girl? How did you get here???".

I also have a few fine memories of my childhood during the elementary school years. In late spring of each year, the entire school will have family picnics with lunch, drinks and snacks in your knapsack. We walked miles to get to the picnic sight while we all sang along with excitement. It is a special occasion when I got to eat boiled eggs, kimbub (rise rolls with veggies and meat), and cookies, and drink soda. Orange soda was my favorite drink and we didn't get a chance to drink that often. Eggs were scarce and expensive at that time and only the middle to upper income families could effort to eat them. My mother never participated in any of these events with me because she had three young ones too look after, but my sister came along few times and, although she beat me quite often, I was so happy she came. Another big day in our school was the gym day competition with Blue team vs. the Red team by each grade levels. This day there would also be a feast with the families and prizes will be given out at the end of the games. I never won anything because I am not good at sports but I still had fun running along with others or sitting out and watching the game.

I remember taking a picture with her on school gym day. Our mother mostly kept a distance from her own children, but she managed to meet a young man whom she thought resembled her long-lost son. I suppose it helped her to fill hollow space in her heart. He frequently visited our home and mother would prepare a nice meal for him. I hated that man, not because he was taking my brother's place, but because of the way he touched me. Whenever I saw him coming up the street, I'd hide behind the dumps on the side of our house or between large drum cans stacked on the property far from the house used for road work. I would wait in silence until I caught a glimpse of him leaving our street. When I'd return home my mother would scorn me for being disrespectful to our guest by disappearing without saying hello.. Sometimes I ran to the field where rustling grasses are thick and tall and I would lay in the stillness, studying at the blue sky and counting the dragon flies flying around me. Maybe because of that memory, the dragonflies are my favorite insects in the whole wide world.

In fact, I got a tattoo of a dragonfly when I was going through a "middle age crisis".

Unfortunately, my mother's adopted son was not the only person who touched me in uncomfortable ways as a child. I was also sexually molested by a young man who lived next door to my family. He was about the same age as my older brother who was taken away to North Korea and I thought of him like my own brother. In those days it was normal for recognizing your neighbors like your own family. We all called everyone "brother, sister, aunt, uncle, granddad and grandma" and we treated each other like family. I don't have a whole lot of memory of the events but I do remember him holding my hand and walking somewhere-I remember the darkened room and him on top of me.

I don't remember whose house it was and I don't even remember getting into the room but remember the terror, feeling like I couldn't breathe, couldn't move,...everything else was blocked out. I had many nightmares and night terrors for the longest time, even as an adult. Each nightmare I was suffocating and move my body, like I was captured in frozen block of ice. Sometimes I would lay with my eyes open but I could not move or make any noise and I was terrified.

Then one night, my family was awoken by loud weeping from next door. I learned later that the young man who molested me (more than once) had died in a truck accident early that evening. He was a construction worker and fell off the back of a dump truck and the driver accidentally put the gear on reverse, stepped on the accelerator and the truck ran over his neck; he was killed instantly. For the longest time, I felt so guilty and scared because I thought my hatred towards him somehow caused his death.

Being beat up and molested was not the only problem I had as a child. I suffered from ulcers, hemorrhoids and internal bleeding. I was scraggy looking and miserable. I missed many school days because as I was sick all the time and I was failing in math. My mother finally took me to the Chinese doctor, who treated me with acupuncture on my belly, both knees and gave us 12 packages of herbal medicine. The medicine seemed to be helping; yet, I was the shortest and the skinniest kid in my class. I barely managed to finish the 6th grade because of illness and lack of financial assistance. In 1950's in Korea there was no full public education like here in America. Everyone had to pay the annual fees, even in elementary school. If anyone wished to send their children to have further education after elementary, they had to pay the high cost of tuition. Only children who had rich parents would dream of going to Jr. High or High School and get to wear fancy uniforms. Most other kids landed in factory jobs or helping out with household chores while parents worked. There was also no such thing as school buses, and we attend school half days on Saturdays. We all had to walk miles to school and back in rain, snow or heat; if the school was too far than you would take the public bus to get to the school.

We had a summer break, but were given homework that required study every day in order to complete the assignments before vacation ended. When I was in elementary school, I was often sent home during the school period to collect the past due school fees. When I would get home, my mother would become stressed out from me asking for money she didn't have and would punish me by hitting me with the bamboo stick, not once but 7 to 10 strikes at a time.

Home was not the only place where I would get hit. Once my 6 grades teacher asked me to stand up in front of the class because I didn't have an answer to his question. When I stood up, he slapped my face so hard he almost knocked me off from the chair while entire class watched in silence. I was more embarrassed than anything else. This may seem absurd, but it was not unusual for students to get physically punished by teachers in those days. If you did not complete your homework on time or did bad on tests, you would get your palms or calf beat with the bamboo ruler. Regrettably, these punishments happened more often to low income class children than the rich kids. The reason being is that rich parents would bribe teachers with envelopes full of money whenever they got a chance. It was a well-known fact that teachers depended on briberies much more than their monthly paychecks.

Through all of this I still had the rebel in me because I resisted to surrender to who everyone thought was the neighborhood bully named "Joung". She was about 3 years older them I was and she was tall, dark skinned with strong features, and just about all of the kids in the street followed her. She lived with her adopted father in a small house, but because of her appearance no kid dared to argue with her or stand up to her. According to my mother, Joung was abandoned by her parents, or maybe they got killed during the war, but the man claimed her as his own child and raised her. I felt bad for her but at the same time, getting beat up at home was enough and I didn't need someone else to order me around for nothing. Not knowing any of this my mother sometimes had her babysit my younger brother and she would always have her stay to have dinner with us. One day she was watching my brother she heard me singing in the back yard. Joung compliment my voice and I told her that I had a song book I cloud loan to her. She then told me she could not read or write because her dad could not afford to send her to school. From there on we became good friends; she was more like a big sister. I often spent the night at her house while her father worked 3rd shift at the local factory. She loved to sing along with me and she memorized many lyrics and tunes so we could sing together. I read many stories for her, and she'd fall asleep before I finished 4-5 pages of the book...I can still remember her face, sound asleep.

Nevertheless, I finally gained my freedom from my sister's abuse, because she got married and moved out of our home when she was 20 years old. On her wedding day, there was a feast prepared in front of our house for family and neighbors. I remembered that my mother prepared a large table for the vagabonds to join celebration, enjoy food and they sang and danced. It's a strange emotion which I could not understand, but there were times that I missed her. In fact, I never once hated her. I just wished that she was more kind and loving towards me and our brother who was taken away. Her husband was born in North Korea, and he escaped from the communist regime during the war. He was nearby a bomb explosion and was severely wounded from particles that penetrated all over his body and was left for dead. Miraculously, he survived and changed his identity and blended in with the South Korean soldiers. After the war ended, he had no home to return to. Somehow, he got to know my father who later hired him at work and looked after him. Eventually he became like one of our family members and married my older sister. He was tall, handsome and loved our family, and unlike my sister, he treated me with kindness. He was smart, a good provider for my sister and a loving husband. They built their own home on the hillside and the garden filled with flowers and vegetables. They had three beautiful children, 2 boys and a girl, and they lived happily ever after like the fairytale story. Oddly, my sister was a loving mother to her children and a good wife to her husband.

By the time I reached age 13, I was working at the pencil factory for sorting out led from the mounds of dirt, sand and rocks. After sorting out led, we would put them in the shifter with a wire net and wash them with water, to prepare for going into the machine that grinds them until it became led powder. The final project for making thin pencil led belonged to professional machine operators. At the end of each day, we all look like cartoon characters, covered with black powder and blinking eyes and we all giggled at each other. Before we left for home, we would wait in line to wash ourselves with the water hose and a bar of soap we shared. I also worked at the sweat shop for ironing clothes, and the clock manufacturer, making cases to help support my family. I often had to take care of my three younger siblings beside working at the factories. As I mentioned earlier my mother suffered a lifelong depression and my father wasn't around very much. My father worked for the city of Incheon; he was in charge of taking care of the wastewater system, and also did the road work for the city as the side job. The pay wasn't good but we were granted free housing throughout the city. The only problem was that my father spent most of his paychecks at the village bars. My mother managed to regroup herself from depression and did odd jobs to help support our family. Having my mother up and about was a huge relief, but her awakening from the depression created other problems.

One day she came home and surprised all of us with a fresh new look. She always had long hair twirled up in bun, as our customary for middle aged women. To our surprise she cut her hair short, and had it permed and styled. She also had makes up on her face with red lipstick and I admit, she looked good. The problem was that she began to spend lot of time taking care of only herself and going out in the evenings. She often bought herself new outfits, and began coming home late at night, and there were some nights that she didn't come home at all. When she did come home, she would tell me about the guys she met at the bars and how she enjoyed the good food and their company. She did not realize that this made me feel sick to my stomach every time she told her stories, and I began to resent her. I am not sure whether my father knew what she was doing or he just didn't care, because he was drunk most of the time when he was not at work. My father must have been a functioning alcoholic because he kept his job until his retirement.

Throughout my childhood I longed for further education. I wanted to live a better life than my parents had, and become somebody that my parents would be proud of, but it seemed to be only a 'pipe dream'. Then one day, I saw an advertisement posted on the telephone pole by the sidewalk. The post was about recruiting young teens who had an interest in continuing education. There were a group of college students who rented the school building on evenings and taught junior high-level education to under-privileged teens at no cost except for the study materials. I was thrilled to spot the information and visited the site to sign up. I was enthralled about learning and loved to study history and the English language. I worked on days and went to school at evenings, but my enthusiasm did not last very long because meeting the financial responsibility for my family grew more important.

When I was about 15 years old, my parents had a big argument because my father got schemed from his business partner whom he did the road work with.; His partner collected all of the money and disappeared. This left my father owing labor workers their paychecks without money to pay them. There were people lined up in front of our house to demand their paycheck. My mother was furious and packed her bag and announced that she was leaving for good and left home. One day turned into weeks and weeks turn into months but we did not hear from our mother, and my father had little to no interest in finding her, and he seldom came home. When our mother left home my brother was about 12, and my two younger sisters were about 9 and 5. I made sure that my siblings went to school every day and left the youngest one with the old lady in our neighborhood to go to work. I made sure that we had food on the table when I came home from school. When my siblings slept, I sat by the window, hoping to hear my mother's footsteps on the porch and open the door.

Several months went by without hearing from her. I began to lose hope and I felt sad for my younger siblings. I started to blame myself for her leaving us and I really wished that I was never born at all. I thought to myself that if I was gone, then she may have had no choice but to come home to her young ones. I felt that my mother would not have left these kids if I wasn't there to care for them. The brooding thoughts of killing myself felt justified; I was a "damaged girl" and as far as I was concerned, I had no future. I thought it would be worth it if I could offer up myself to salvage our family and protect my siblings. Days went by and I finally got the courage to purchase a bottle of rat poison. I heard people committed suicide by drinking rat poison and I thought it would surely work for me. That evening I made a good dinner, watched my siblings enjoy the meals I prepared, cleaned up and tucked them to sleep. I sat beside them for a while and when I heard the gentle sounds of their breathing, I carefully rolled up the rat poison in an old newspaper and head out to the local park. When I got to the Inchon's most famous park called 'Freedom Park', the misty sky of an early summer shadowed over the horizon.

The freedom park was located on top of the low mountain side, a place well known for a large copper statue of General MacArthur. Wearing sunglasses and holding his binocular in his right hand was the trade mark of his statue. He stood tall and there were images of infantry carved on the stone at the bottom looking over the port, to remind us of the day of his landing to save us. I remember the sound of insects buzzing in the mist, looking at thickening leaves fading into the misty rain. It must be the rain coming because there was hardly anyone around at the park. The reason I chose this place was because I thought my death needed to be publicized, otherwise my mother would never find out. I walked slowly with a million thoughts racing through my mind as I came in front of public bathroom.

I open the door to see if anyone was in the bathroom but did not hear or see anyone, and it was dead quiet. I went in one of the stalls and gulp down the bottle of rat poison to the last drop. I honestly don't even remember what the poison tasted like. After drinking the poison, I threw the bottle into the trash and went outside, found a bench and sat, waiting to die. I felt my stomach growling and I could taste bitterness in my mouth with slight numbness on my tongue. I tilted my head back, closed my eyes and prayed "please let me die". I felt soft rain drops paddling on my face but for some reason, I didn't feel like I was going to die. I stood up from the bench, wiped my face with both hands and started to walk aimlessly until I came upon the overpass, a bridge called rainbow bridge. This bridge was built through the hillside of a low mountain where the rainbow shaped tunnel passed underneath and the traffic constantly passed through beneath the narrowed tunnel. This bridge was well known for suicide jumpers. If you jump from this bridge you were likely to smash your skull on the asphalt or pavement, or hit by one of the passing cars and you would surely die. I remembered reading newspapers about many suicide jumpers on this bridge and the bridge earned nick name for "the bridge of death". The bridge does not look so high but there had been many adults who have jumped off and died and I was less than 5 ft tall and weighed about 85 pounds. However, the thought of gruesome death horrified me. I was trembling with the fear; my teeth were crunching together and my legs were shaking uncontrollably. At the end of the bridge I found the little opening and I squeezed myself through, stood on the edge and looked down. The street looked dampen and cars with headlights were passing through the tunnel. Thoughts rushed through my mind "you have to do it, it's the only way you can save your family, take a leap of faith and just jump", "Just take one step further and it will be all over". There, I looked up at the mournful sky; I closed my eyes, took one deep breath, covered my face with both hands and took one foot off into the air..... It felt like everything was turning in a slow motion as I fell until my body hit the ground. The beastly sound of bones crashing to the ground was only way I can describe what I heard. Unspeakable and horrendous pain rushed through my body as I tumbled on to the wet asphalt. I tried to lift my body from the ground but I couldn't move....I howled and moaned like a wounded animal. The street lights were beaming through the drizzling rain and I could see my dismantled legs and the blood spreading on the wet black asphalt. I saw people gathering around me, but their faces disappeared like bubbles into the thickening air.....

Later, I was told that I was in a coma for five days at the city hospital. At that time in Korea, there was no health care system, or at least I don't know anything about it. Most of the hospitals are private facilities and you have to pay cash up front to get any kind of treatment. The city hospital is run by the government and they provide low cost treatment for low income families, but this comes with poorly managed treatment, with limited doctors and nurses. I recall hearing the rain drops dropping into the bucket from a hole in the tin roof. Drip, drip, drip....

The clouds were slowly brushed away as the warm sun glared at my face. I felt the last few drops of warm rain falling onto my face wake me up. I slowly opened my eyes, and there was my mother crouched over me crying; It was her tear drops on my face that woke me up from the deep sleep. I could hardly move my body from the waist down. The casts on both legs were all the way up to my thighs. Soon after I regained consciousness, the doctor in a white coat walked in with the nurse. The nurse wore a white A-line dress, white shoes with white stockings and a white nurse's cap with the black stripes.

My mother whispered "here comes Dr. Beck (백), he is the medical director of this hospital". "So, she woke up" the doctor said in a monotone voice looking at my mother. He came one step closer to look into my eyes and listen to my heart with the stethoscope. I still remember his white coat smelt like cigarette smoke and he appeared to be in his fifties with fading pepper gray hair. His eye glasses hung on the bridge of his wide nose and he looked over to me with the stern face. "It's going to be a long recovery young lady" he said as he walked out, leaving the nurse behind him to check the wounds on my ankles. My mother said that she was living near Seoul, working for a family as a house keeper and heard the news about my incident. I later learned this was not exactly why she left out family-- I found the letter written by my mother to her long-lost lover from her childhood. He had been a servant of her family and became rich after the Korean war was over. She somehow reunited with him during the time she was gone, but left him after my fall because her family needed her, I needed her. The newspaper indicated that either I was pushed by someone or I accidentally slipped off from the small opening on the bridge. No one suspected that it was a suicide attempt and there was no investigation of any kind. Ironically, no one found the suicide note in my pocket, and my parents never knew what really happened. People were assumed that it was an accident and I didn't bother to tell anyone otherwise because I was just glad that my mother came   home   to   stay.

The wounds on my both ankles were severe and I was in agonizing pain. Both of my legs were broken and my ankles had been crushed. The doctor had to cut out holes in the casts to expose my ankle area to be treated daily. The flesh on both ankles was gashed and the bone lay bare.

The summer heat began to climb each day, and with the lack of a cooling system at the city hospital and no proper medication, the wounded area started to decay. The noise from the metal table wheeling into the room by the nurse made cringe with fear. She would have some surgical tools on the metal table and say "okay it's time" as she scraped off the rotting flash along with shattered pieces of bone, without any pain killers. If I screamed, I would get no treatment. I'd cover my face, bite my teeth and cry in silence as streams of tears rolled down to my ears. I'd be drenched with sweat from agonizing pain, so bad that I thought and wished I was better off dead. After several long summer months in the hospital bed, Autumn finally arrived and the long and painful recovery process continued, albeit a bit less agonizing. The city hospital was short staffed and it was the family's responsibility to care for their loved one's for daily hygiene. The nurses and medical

staff only provided limited

medical care and treatments. My mother could not visit me as often as she would like to because the responsibility of taking care of the younger children at home. I only remember my father visiting me once at the hospital. Maybe he did more, but I just don't remember seeing him more than once. My older sister had her own family to care for but she visited me few times with her little boy, and he was handsome just like his dad.

Chapter Three

I had some other visitors while I was at inpatient, people from factory that I worked, previous school friends and people from our neighborhood. Among those visitors I was especially glad to see my old English teacher Mr. Park (college student) from the night school I briefly attended a year ago. He was shocked to read the newspaper about his old student and came to see how I was doing. Mr. Park was liked by many students but especially by girls. He had a bit of a feminine look but he was kind, had a good heart and was majoring business management at a well-known college in Seoul. He brought me books to read, snacks to munch on and sometimes he even washed my hair for me. Mr. Park continued to visit me at least 2-3 nights a week, and soon I became dependent on his support. I enjoyed reading books he brought for me and loved having clean hair. Who wouldn't want attention when you are bound to a hospital bed and your own family is too busy to care for you.

I did have roommates, four of them altogether. I don't remember much of anything about three of them, but one particular woman I shared a room with I looked up to like a big sister. She was in her late 20's and she has been in the hospital for a few months. I learned that she attempted suicide by drinking a bleach kind of substance, which melted her throat lining to her esophagus. She was lucky to be alive but she could no longer swallow anything. She constantly spit using a can and fed herself a through thin hose that was attached to her stomach. She was scheduled for the very first experimental surgery at that hospital to repair her damaged throat. She explained to me that she agreed to the experimental surgery in exchange for covering the hospital bills. I asked her why she tried to take her own life and she told me she thought she had nothing to live for adding, "I was given up right after my birth". She continued on and explained that she was adopted by family who abused her emotionally and physically. As an adult she fell in love with a man who later revealed that he was married and had children. She was broken hearted and lost all hope for living. She had no one to visit her and I felt bad for her, but soon we became good roommates. Once she told me she really wished that she could have an orange popsicle, soI asked Mr. Park if he could bring her the popsicle on his next visit, which he did and I shared with her. She very much enjoyed the taste and spit it out into the can until it was gone, and we both laughed.

As Mr. Park's visits became more frequent, he would stay later at nights. Then he began to try and force himself on me. I tried to push him away but I was also afraid someone was going to find out and I would be ashamed and may even get kicked out of the hospital. The room I shared with four other patients, and the space was divided with only curtains. l lay helplessly with the heavy casts up to my thighs; his forceful habits continued each time he visited. I felt ashamed, dirty and humiliated, but I was too scared to say anything to anyone. I knew very well that in our culture people would blame the victim and I would be ridiculed. It would be his word against mine and no one would believe me. It is just how things were back in the days. I liked Mr. Park and appreciated him very much, but being forced into sex in a hospital bed with casts on was not how I want to be treated as human being.

The day I was being discharged from the hospital, the treating doctor informed my parents that I would never walk again. My father came to the hospital on my discharge date and brought me back home, still with my casts on. When I arrived home, I saw a wooden bed by the window which my father himself built with the scrap wood. In the corner of the room I saw an old rusty wheel chair someone has donated awaiting me. The days seemed long, and nights felt like eternity. I wrote many poems and short stories for time to pass. I also read many books, mostly western nobles which translated to Korean language. My favorite book was Sherlock Holmes. I could get lost in his mysterious narration, it helped me to escape from the reality. At times I also loved reading poems written by Robert Frost; his portrayal of rural life in England fascinated me. Unfortunately, not long after I came home my mother start staying out again. One morning I had to drag myself to the kitchen, which was an outdoor cooking room attached to the house with a dirt floor. I start the fire on a small stove with some sticks and wood chips to fix breakfast, packed lunch and sent my siblings off to school because my mother didn't come home the night before.

As the time past, I felt that my legs were getting stronger. There was no follow up appointment with the hospital to take off the cast and neither of my parents had a plan to take me back to the hospital. One day when I felt good enough, I found the scissors and cut the casts off myself, which took me awhile. The appearance of my legs after cutting off the casts was not what I hoped to see. The looks of my ankles devastated me. Both ankles were deformed, bulging and crooked. Below my knee to the ankles looked much shorter than I remembered. I stood up but to my dismay instantly I fell to the floor. There was absolutely no strength in my legs, none whatsoever; I couldn't feel a thing.

I remembered overhearing my mother's whisper to my brother-in-law who was visiting us "the doctor said she will never walk again" "I am afraid that she is going to try to kill herself". The thought of spending the rest of my life in a wheelchair devastated me and I was angry at myself for being in that situation. Sometimes at night while everyone was asleep, I would drag my body out to the backyard and cry out to the heavens. I was not a Christian and never read the bible. I only went to the church once as child with the neighborhood kids because I heard that they were giving away pastries during Christmas season. My mother was a Buddhist and I was not allowed to visit church because they served a "foreign god" from the western culture. In spite of my mother's warning, I snuck out of the house and went anyway. If I had any street smart, even a common sense, I would have eaten the pastries before I got home, but I brought them home to share with my younger brother who told out mother. I got beaten when my mother found out that I went to the church. The pastries were so sweet, delicious and it was well worth it for little pain. In light of all of this, I heard that God was the creator of all things and I thought that if he is powerful enough, then he certainly must have power to make me walk again. I cried out to the night sky and asked God in heaven to give me the strength to stand up. After many long and treacherous attempts, I was able to stand up holding onto the fence. I asked my father to build me crutches with scrap wood, and after several months of practice, I could take small steps with support of crutches. I worked very hard, and a few years later I had gained enough strength and capacity to walk again, though I was limping. The injury had caused my left leg to be shorter than the right one because of the impact on my left ankle. My waist was crooked to the right side and even my belly button is shifted to the right side and still is. Nevertheless, I had a strong belief that the God of heaven and earth made me walk again. My legs were skinny like twigs, ankles were deformed and I walked with the limp for the longest time, but I was grateful that I could walk again.

Mr. Park continued to visit me at home after discharged from the hospital and he became sort of like a family member. My mother welcomed him because she had one less thing to worry about when he was around, expecting him to take care of me. Soon after I started to walk again, I found out that I was pregnant for the first time, but Mr. Park said that he was not ready to be a father. He was also upset and fearful of disappointing his parents who has high expectation of him. One night he took me out; we got on the bus and we got off at the back alley in different city. He then took me into a building where I was strapped onto a metal bed and an unlicensed practitioner performed an abortion on me without proper anesthetic. I felt every part of my being ripped away as she scraped the fetus from my womb. I screamed and screamed but no one was there to help me. The nurse assisting the doctor shoved cloth into my mouth and shouted "shut up you little tramp", "you ought to be ashamed of yourself for being pregnant at all!!" Mr. Park left me there, hurrying out before the procedure began, and returned just after the procedure was done to take me back to my parents. I was bleeding heavily and in pain but we had to walk the rest of way once we got off the bus. People might ask, "why didn't you leave him? why did you keep accepting him?" Well, then we can ask the same questions to all battered wives and girlfriends. I just accepted the situation because I felt there was no way out and in my feeble mind, he was the only one who cared for me and I belonged to him. I was a damaged girl at age 15 and I didn't know how else to fix the problem. I didn't know any better. I had no one to talk to, and no one would understand what I was going through. I was suffering from depression and anxiety all throughout my life, I had no idea how to express my perplexed condition to someone or anyone for that matter. I was also fearful of social stigma and being labeled as "lunatic" and probably sent away to Asylum Island. I've seen mentally ill people who were outcast from the society and alienated from their own family. There was no proper mental health treatment in Korea, and in those days people who were thought to be crazy were cast away too far off places. No one would talk to them or care for them and they would inevitably die from hunger, physical ailments and even get killed by the cruelness of the people. I had never heard of such thing as birth control pills and we didn't have primary care physicians.

Be that as it may, when I turned 18, I got pregnant again. I had no sense of self-worth and I was submissive to whatever Mr. Park desired. Despite that, I told Mr. Park, I was pregnant again and he repeated the same story, saying that he was afraid he would disappoint his family. He said that telling his parents about having a child was not an option. This time I told him that I was not about to get another abortion because the horrendous memory of the steel bed has and will continue to haunt me for the rest of my life. I was also old enough to know that the unborn child's life was just as important as my own breath. Then he promised to find a job in another city further down the south, and he told me he would contact me when he got situated. After he left, I received a couple of letters from him without any sign of him coming back or having me move to wherever he lived. My family then decided to move to another village further from the city, because they were ashamed of me for having a child out of wedlock. My family moved to a small hut which was converted from an old chicken coop in the outskirt of Incheon. My father practically stayed at his job where he had the sleeping quarters and my mother was out most of the time. There was no running water in the house and no electricity. We used oil lamps and candles for lights and cooked from the coal or burned woods in a circled rock pit in a dirt room, and we had only one room for everyone to sleep, eat and gather. The water was drawn from the community water well and either carried on my head or on my shoulder to use for cooking and washing. I did the laundry by the well only at night when no one will notice me. I spent most of my time taking care of my brother and sisters and made sure they were fed, got to school on time and did their homework. I felt ashamed when I heard that my brother or sisters were teased by other kids in the village, because they had sister who got "knocked up".

In March 1966, I gave birth to a boy and we named him Jinsug. My mother didn't come home the night before, but she arrived a few hours before I gave birth and she was able to assist. She cut the umbilical cord and wrapped him with an old cut out sheet. The baby was perfect and he looked so beautiful. My parents hardly spoke to each other, or to me before and after the baby was born. My father refused to look at the baby, took a long sight and walked out of the room. Two weeks after Jinsug was born, my mother somehow found the address of Mr. Park's parents. She said that I should take the baby and give it to them and start a new life. I understood that she was just wanted me to have a better life, but giving up my child was not in the cards. Maybe I was being selfish but I refused her advice; which made her angry to the point where she attacked me physically. Next thing I knew, I was on the bus with my mother and Jinsug heading out to Mr. Park's parent's home in the city Incheon. Incheon, now officially the Incheon Metropolitan City, is located in northwestern South Korea, bordering Seoul and Gyeonggi to the west. Inhabited since the Neolithic, Incheon was home to just 4,700 people when it became an international port in 1883. Today, about 3 million people live in the city with the one of the largest international airports in the world.

As we were heading out to Dowha Dong (city name) in Incheon, my mother continued telling me that I should leave the baby and start fresh, because if I keep the baby, I have no hope for the future. After getting off from the bus we walked at least a half mile and stood in front of the Mr. Park's home. The double wooden door with heavy large ring shape knocker seemed scary. The wooden door would lead to the court yard and then to the main house. I was trembling with fear how of they were going to react to the news as I heard the door open with a squeaky noise. The face of a teenage girl poked out and then turn around, calling out in loud voice, "mom, there are some people out here!" I could hear a woman clearing her throat and "who are they?" The girl left the door open slightly, walking back to the main room as she responds "I don't know". I was standing behind my mother but I could hear someone coming towards the door and I felt dizzy, like I was about to faint. The middle age woman with slanted eyes and buck teeth stopped and pushed the door little further. "Okay, who are you people and what do you want?" she questioned, when she saw me holding the baby. Mr. Park's parents were in total shock and his mother fell to the floor and hysterically wept, like someone just had died. Surprisingly Mr. Park's father seemed to be accepting of the situation, quickly without any squabble. He in fact appeared to be happy to hold his first born grandson whom was the spitting image of his son even to the little mole on his left ear. After the shock of the situation was over, Mr. Park's mother regrouped herself and told me that it was up to me to whether to stay with them or leave, but leave baby with them. I decided to stay with my baby, and my mother headed out for her home in the village.

Before I go on - It sounds as though my mother was a monster, but she really wasn't. She suffered unimaginable emotional pain all throughout her life. She was the only child to her wealthy parents and grew up in a beautiful home with servants to care for her. Her father held third highest rank in the King's palace; she was loved and never needed or wanted for anything. When she was 16 she got engaged to my father (arranged by her parents) but she was already in love with one of their servant boys who was about the same age as she was. Although my father was handsome, educated and the descendent from a royal family, she could not surrender her heart to him. I was told that when my mother disappeared at the time that I jumped off the bridge, she reunited with the same servant boy whom she was in love with when she was a teenager. That servant boy became a successful business man who owned one of the largest metal/steel corporation in Korea's capital city Seoul. However, to my mother's dismay, he was married and had three sons. Regardless of the situation, they tried to rekindle the love they longed for and that was the real reason why my mother left us. The short-lived love affair had to end when I threw myself off from the rainbow bridge. So you see, my mother did sacrifice herself for our family and lived the rest of her life in misery and I feel I am responsible for her misery.

Back to my story at Mr. Park's home. A few weeks later he returned home and we all lived under the same roof. Mr. Park and his family instantly fell in love with our newborn baby boy, but they all kept their distance from me, including Mr. Park. They treated me as though I was their servant who cooks, cleans, washes their clothes (by hand) and waited on them. Mr. Park had three sisters and one older brother. His brother worked for a cargo ship down in the south province called Pusan, which is now called Busan Metropolitan city; the second most popular city after Seoul. His oldest sister was married and lived in Seoul and his two younger sisters who were in high school lived at home. His sisters were cruel, controlling and hated me, believing I was a stumbling block to their brother's future. It was customary in our culture to serve sister-in laws. I washed their menstrual clothes by hand and boiled them in an old pot with a bleach kind of substance to remove the stain. After washing was done, I would dry them, fold them neatly and place them in their drawers for their next use. Once I wore a skirt that fell above my knees and I thought I look pretty decent but Bong song's mother didn't approve. "What the hell you are wearing now? How dare you wear such slutty looking clothes at my home?! Do you think you are some kind of teenager or something?". She threw a pair of her old elastic waist under pants in front of me "you better wear this under the skirt, oh lord, I am so disgusted". I looked like a total idiot with an old traditional under pants that reaches my ankle with the short skirt. When Bong song came home, he avoided eye contact with me and went to greet his parents. You may wonder why I wouldn't just leave – but where would I go? In those days, women weren't counted for much, especially in my situation. I was uneducated, unwed with a child and there were no decent opportunities for women like me, not to mention I would have to leave my son with them.

While I was living with Mr. Park's family his mother took a trip to Busan to visit her older son. As I mentioned, he worked for a merchant cargo ship for imports/exports and he was out of the country several months at a time. While she was visiting him, she had the chance to attend a large expo for new marketing products. Busan is the economic, cultural and educational center of southeastern Korea, and has become Korea's busiest port and 9th busiest in the world. She was proud to attend the expo and brought home some of the new trends in the market. She brought beautiful pastille green, orange and yellow plastic sandals for her three daughters, pretty underwear and other goodies for each family member, but not a single thing for me. My feeling was hurt, although I felt

more humiliated than anything else, I
didn't have the time to dwell on this"
because, I hardly had time to go to the
weekly bath at the town bath facility. At
that time there was not too many people
had a bathtub or shower in their own
home. Most people will go to the "bath
house" for weekly baths and during the
rest of the week we used wash pan for
daily clean. Also, Jinsug was a fussy baby
and I had to cradle him many of the
nights for him to sleep. Although this
was a lot of work, it was the only time I
could hold him and feel the comfort and
hold his little hands.

Mr. Park spent most of his time
away from home. I am embarrassed to
say this but when he did spend the night
at home, he was sexually abusive to me,
so much so that I don't want to talk
about the details. Eventually, he met a
girl from his work and they nestled into
an apartment on the other side of the
town. Mr. Park worked in the financial
department of Dae Han transportation
and she was the secretary. Obviously,

she dressed professional, a 'night and day' differences compared with me. His mother was rather proud of her son's infidelity and often visited them. She openly bragged about how tall and beautiful her son's mistress was, and since I am not married to him "he was not committing any adultery" and therefore I had no right to be jealous. I began to write a journal about my grief-stricken life and hid it underneath the large rice box in the corner of kitchen. I always like to write and writing was one of ways express my deepest thoughts and feeling that I could not share with anyone. The kitchen was the place where I spent the majority of my time. Mr. Park's mother even calls me "hey, girl in the kitchen, bring me a drink for me, would you?" I was the last one to eat at meal time after serving everyone else; I'd get the leftover scoop of rice and the soup and sit at the corner of the table, but most of the times I eat in the kitchen alone.

One day when I was gone to the open market for groceries, one of Bong Song's younger sisters discovered my journal and gave it to her mother. When I returned home from grocery shopping, I found his mother sitting at the middle of 'marue' which is the hardwood floor between bedrooms and she was enraged. I saw my journal torn up and thrown all over the floor. I was called into the room and as I kneeled down, she slapped me across my face. She began to lecture me about my duties at her home. She made me promise that I would never again write any type of journal, or I will be forced out of their home without my baby. I heard her daughters giggling in the courtyard as I returned to the kitchen to prepare for dinner. After a long silent cry in the kitchen as I was preparing for dinner, I heard the baby crying in my room. When I went to feed him, something sparked in my head "take the baby and run". Suddenly, I found the courage I needed. I took the little money I had left over from the grocery shopping; I wrapped the baby with a small blanket and grabbed the diaper bag. I peeked outside through the sliding door and saw the girls had gone into their room and noon was in the courtyard. I open the sliding door slowly, walked out of the room quietly and as soon as I left the front gate, I started to run with my baby. I wasn't sure where I was going, but I just knew I had to get away from them.

Chapter Four

I got on the first bus that came to the bus stop without looking where it was going. When the bus reached its final destination, I got off and found I was by the beach with a park where people visit to spend the leisure times. I walked with Jinsug on my arms for a while and then sat on the beach and watched the baby playing with the sand. I heard people's laughter from the distance; I looked around I saw a little girl on the swing set and the couple were chatting and laughing. As I thought to myself, "they are so lucky" and "what is wrong with me?" when I saw the glimpse of a familiar face from the direction where the couple was chatting. Suddenly I realized that the man I was looking at from the distance was Bong song and his girlfriend with a child. He must have seen me too because, he quickly walked over to me. He stood in front of me and slapped my face with such force it almost knocked me to the ground. He began to accuse me of spying on him and shouted that I was an embarrassment in his life. His girlfriend was hysterical and he embraced her, then walked away disappearing from my sight. He had no idea that I was running away from his home. He just thought I followed him to spy on him; besides he would never have figured it out or imagined that I had the guts to run away. I sat on the beach for hours until the baby started to cry. We got on the bus again but I didn't know where else to go... but one thing I knew for sure was that I definitely didn't want to go back to Bong song's house. The next bus was going to a port by the sea. I got on the bus again with Jinsug to head out to the port. I saw people getting on ferries to small islands and I decided to get on one of the ferries. The trip landed me on the island called Young jongdo. I have never been there and I certainly didn't know anyone, not to mention I had no idea how I was going to survive with a baby.

Not knowing what to do, I walked and walked... I finally stopped at one of the small houses and knocked at the door.

The sun was slowly setting over the hill
and we were hungry. I saw an old man
open the door and I explained to him that
we needed a place for lodging. He said
that he had no room in his place but there
was a nice young couple who owned a
large farm about a mile away, and they
may need a helping hand. I walked again,
carrying Jinsug on my back and followed
the directions that were given by the kind
old man. We finally came up on the big
house with the large yard, and I could
smell the traditional Korean miso soup
someone was cooking. There, I met the
nicest couple who was kind enough to
take us in for an exchange of helping
them on the soybean farm. They offered
for us to have dinner with them and I was
thankful for soup, rice, kimchi and other
dishes they offered. The baby could have
rice mixed with soup and I breast fed him
at night. The couple owned the large
farming land and had cows, a pet dog and
enough rooms in the outer house for
helpers. They let me stay in one of their
helper's quarters and I was able to work
on the soybean farm with my baby on my
back. I also helped prepare meals for the

household and did the dishes. I enjoyed
the smell of the dirt and pulling weeds off
from the ground, it calmed my nerves.
The air felt fresh, even though the breeze
often would smell of the sea. I had no one
to belittle me and humiliate me as long as
I did my work as I was told, things were
peaceful. When evening would come all
helpers sat down and ate together like a
family.

They all loved my baby, including
the lady of the house because they did
not have any children. We stayed there
for about four months and although
farming was a hard labor, nothing
compared to the abuse I got from Bong
song's family. I was at my peace and
happy to be free from emotional abuse.
The farm owners were kind-hearted
people, especially the lady of the house,
and I got along well with their helpers.
However, one evening the lady of the
house came over to helper's quarters and
wanted to have a talk with me. She said
that she sensed I was in some sort of
trouble, but she also saw me as a young

woman with potential for success in life.
She advised me to return to the main
land to face the problem "whatever that
might be" and start a fresh life. She
sounded sincere and since she was older
me, I decided to take her advice and go
back to Incheon- but not to the Bong
song's house.

A few weeks later I said farewell to
the island family, got on the ferry and
returned to the main land. The lady of the
house on the island gave me enough
money to take care of me and my child
while I figured it out what to do next.
When we got to Inchon port, I decide to
visit my parents and let them know that
we were okay. My parents were glad that
we were alive but also upset with me for
running away with my child. I told my
mother about the abuse that I had to
endure, and I was looking to go to Seoul
to find work. Then, early the next
morning to my surprise, Mr. Park rushed
into my parent's home and took the baby
and literally dragged me back to his

parent's home. My mother said that she contacted him to let him know that I was back in Incheon because "it was only the right thing to do" and I need to return to Bong song's home "because it's where you belong. ".

Mr. Park's family treated me even worse than before, because they thought I deserved punishment for endangering their grandchild's welfare. I had to deal with his sister's smirking and sarcastic remarks and the unending scorn from his mother. The house chores got heavier with piling up laundry and hours spent sewing stuff from the oldest daughter and aunt (mother's sister). I looked a mess, unkempt and lingering tiredness from lack of sleep and nutrition. Mr. Park must have been feeling bad for me because he bought me 2 yards of cotton fabric with the floral print and said "made yourself a dress, would you? that outfit you are wearing looks ridiculous". I used to make dresses out of old fabrics for my younger sister by hand and she wore them proudly to school. The design of the dress was something I made up in my head without any drawings and I cut them just following my instinct and I loved the outcome.

It was a white sundress with red pleats on the bottom and a red flower sewed on to the top left below the shoulder, and it was beautiful I thought. I was so grateful that Mr. Park thought about me and bought me fabric and I was excited thinking about the design. I ask his mother if I could use her sewing machine to make myself a dress. She had a sewing machine that had the handle on the right side and you would turn with the one hand and use the other hand to sew, while you squat on the floor. His mother became irate and actually foamed at the corner of her mouth as she fell to the floor and let out an awful scream at her son. "How dear you my son! I raised you to honor your parents and this is what I get?? You never bought me a single yard of fabric in my entire life and yet, you bought her fabric? that worthless piece shit?!" She began to wail just like the first time she found out about her grandson. Mr. Park knelt down on the floor and begged her for forgiveness like I have never seen before. He even cried as he tried to comfort her, and assured her that this would never happen again. After that

episode, Mr. Park avoided me with all his
effort and his mother hated me with all of
her might.

Soon I begin to experience
migraines and severe chest pains
accompanied by nausea and vomiting.
Eventually the migraines turned into
nightmares/night terrors and into
psychotic breakdowns. After many
episodes I was fatigued and had no
energy left in me. Mr. Park's mother
consulted with a medium, who told her
that I was possessed by an evil spirit. The
medium advised her to place a knife
under my pillow to break the evil spirit,
but of course it didn't work and I was not
in any shape to tend to their family. The
unexpected situation scared Mr. Park, and
he asked his mother to take me to the
doctor. He whispered to her saying
"mother, we need her to do your chores,
so please take her to the doctor." Later
that afternoon she returned from an
outing and threw 2 tablets of aspirin into
the kitchen where I was standing. She
yelled into the kitchen and said "take that

and stop saying your head hurts, I am sick of hearing it". But the aspirin didn't make any difference. She finally took me to the clinic where the doctor gave me a shot, but it also didn't do anything for me. She then took me to the Chinese doctor who diagnosed me with the "aching heart" (ha ha, funny but it's true). I understand now that I was probably suffering from a major depression with psychotic episodes and anxiety with the panic symptoms due to the stress.

The Chinese doctor prescribed 12 large packets of herbal medicine, one packet for each day to use. The medicine had to be boiled and simmered in a special clay pot at low temperature for at least 5-6 hours until it turned into a thick, dark and bitter liquid just enough for a one cup. Since I had no energy to get up, Mr. Park's mother had no choice but to prepare the medicine for me and I could hear her grunting and muttering words I couldn't quite understand while she did so. One morning I had forced myself up to use the bathroom and spotted that she was boiling my medicine in a pot that I used for boiling her daughters menstrual cloths. It was disgusting to see my medicine was boiling from the same pot. But, regardless of how it was prepared, I drank and slowly got well.

The following autumn, Mr. Park's parents decided to wed us for the sake of their grandchild and have us move out of their home. Mr. Park said that he broke it off with his girlfriend and the child was not his. Before the wedding, his parents decided to renovate the house and hired one person for masonry work and I was the only helper. I had to carry bricks, dirt, and cement bags on my head from the street to their house which was on the hillside. I learned to mix red dirt with the chapped straws to paste on walls, help put bricks in rows and cover with wet cement for the final project. My hands were chapped, fingers were cracked and skin on my face was dried and peeling. When the renovation was completed, there were only a few weeks left before the wedding. Mr. Park's mother ordered me to prepare the food for the wedding party, which would be followed by the wedding ceremony at the wedding house.

Of-course there were neighbors who helped preparing non-perishable foods and I made final food prep u until the morning of the wedding day. In spite of everything, the day of the wedding, I had my hair and makeup done at the salon next to the wedding house. When I opened my eyes after hair and makeup was done, I saw someone else in the mirror. "That's not me" I thought, I could not believe my eyes how different I looked. Everyone said that I looked "beautiful"..... After the ceremony was over, we returned home and the first word's out of Mr. Park's mother's mouth were "don't act like you are some kind of new bride, go change your clothes and help out in the kitchen and of course I did. On the wedding night Mr. Park, now my husband, passed out from drinking too much rice wine and I slept on the other side of the room with baby.

My life was little at ease once we moved out of his parent's home. Although my mother-in-law often made unannounced visits and I still had to answer to her, they were not in my face every minute or hour of the day. Though my husband didn't care for me much, I had a place to eat and sleep, without being belittled by his family.

The following year I gave birth to another boy whom we named Jingewn. I gave birth at home, but this time with a midwife's assistance. Unlike his brother Jinsuk's feminine look, Jingewn looked more like his uncle (Bong Song's brother) who had a more of manly appearance. After recuperating from giving birth, I visited the beauty salon and styled my hair and learned how to put make up on my face. I want to recapture the look I saw in the mirror on my wedding day, and I felt happy with my own reflection. The rumors begin spread at my husband's work that his wife was "beautiful". I kept my hopes up that someday he would notice me and pay attention to me like he paid attention to other women. I know that he was seeing other women, even after we got married. He often didn't come home and when he did the next day, he would pull out used lipstick from his pocket and ask me "do you want this? She only used it a couple of times". I was angry inside, felt nauseous and want to throw up, but I didn't show any emotion. I found out that some of my neighborhood ladies were taking ballroom dancing lessons and one day they asked me if I want to come along with them. It got me curious and I thought that my husband may notice me if I learned how to dance and be more sociable like all the other women he associated with.

My life was getting better, but I had to go on and wreck it all. One evening, I went out with Sonja, the wife of the building owner who lived next door. She often went out to the dance hall, but her husband thought she was going out to play cards with other ladies. He was a gentleman, trustworthy, and I never saw them fight or even argue with each other. He came home every evening like clockwork and I didn't understand "how it could be?". Sonja's mother-in-law was also nice and she liked me because I often shared fresh Kimchi with her. One evening she agreed to baby sit my two kids so I could go out with Sonja to "play cards", she said "you need to get out of the house sometimes, you are so young and cooped up in a house too much". It was so nice to know that not every mother in law is like Bong song's mother but, stupid, stupid of me....what was I thinking going out at night?. It was just my luck, when I came back home from the dancing lesson late that evening, both kids were sleeping but my husband was home, brooding with anger. Honestly, I did enjoy the dancing lesson, but needless to say that he was furious. He became violent, beat me up and accused me for cheating on him. He said that I was an unfit mother and a "dirty whore" and he could no longer live with the "filthy" woman and "we are done". Oh, I did not tell you this, but unfortunately it wasn't the only time he hit me. He'd hit me when

I returned home a little late from visiting my parents. Sometimes he undressed me and stripped of my panties to make sure that I wasn't with anyone. The next morning, he dragged me by my hair and took me to the local law office. My face was bruised and still had the blood stain on the corner of my mouth, but everyone looked the other way.

Divorce was a simple procedure in those days in Korea. Woman had no voice, nor power to dispute anything and it was all up to the mercy of husband for whatever and however he decided to say. The fact that my family never stood up for me or defended me any time also made it easy for Bong song to get what he wanted. He called up his family to come pick up the kids and the divorce papers were quickly prepared right at the lawyer's office and he forced me to seal the paper with the stamp (everyone had a personal stamp instead of signature). Just like that, after all the effort, heartache, sweat and tears... it was finished and we were divorced. He took away my visitation

Autobiography by Un Chu Lee-
Hoyle

rights with our kids and his family brought the moving truck and took away most of the furniture. Our older son Jinsuk was about 3 years old and Jingewn was barely a year old and I was still breast feeding him.

I was about lose my mind; I cried for days with no sleep or food, but there was nothing I could do to change the situation. I couldn't imagine living life without my kids or husband. He abused me in many ways but he was the first and the only man that I relied and depended on since I was 15 years old. Sonja, my next-door neighbor who introduced me to dancing lessons, watched helplessly as the situation unfolded. She said that she felt responsible for what was happening to me. My breasts were swollen like melons for lack of feeding the baby and it was awfully painful. I felt that the purpose in my life had been stripped away and I had no reason to live. Sonja often sat beside me and tried to comfort me, but there wasn't much she can do to ease my situation.

One evening, I got up and walked miles, stopping at every drug store to buy sleeping pills. In those days you could buy just about any kind of drug without a prescription, and there were drug stores on every street corner. However, sleeping pills were potent and people used them for suicide. The drug doctors had a strict policy for selling sleeping pills and you can only get 2-3 pills from each store. I walked a couple of miles at least to buy a handful of pills, and then I came home and took them with a glass of Ginseng rum. The Ginseng rum was a strong homemade hard liquor, which I prepared for special occasions for my husband.

I have no recollection of what happened after I drank the glass of ginseng rum mixed with the sleeping pills. Sonja said that she found me unconscious, called a taxi and took me to the clinic. She said that I remained unconscious or sleeping for 2-3 days; I don't remember going to the clinic or coming home. Sonja said that she contacted my husband and asked for help but he wished not to be involved and told her "it is not my problem". After I was discharged from the clinic, I stayed in my room like a ghost.... If it wasn't for my friend Sonja I probably have died and probably would have been better off. Sonja attended to me for several days, day after day she encouraged me to eat or drink like I was her own sister. I often wonder where she is today.... By that time, my parents pretty much had given up on me, because I do not remember anyone visiting me except my youngest sister. The months went by and I received 15,000 won (approximately $15.00 American dollars) from my ex-husband for the divorce settlement. I could no longer afford to live in the apartment without a job, and I moved in with my parents and gave the settlement money to my mother. By that time my father was retired from his city job and he was able to build a suitable house in the hillside on the outskirts of Incheon with help of his old colleagues. It was ten times better than the converted chicken coop for sure, and I was happy for them.

Soon after I moved in with my parents, my mother contacted the marriage broker and set me up with the couple of meetings. I had no interest in meeting anyone but I met them out of respect for mother's effort. However, the two meetings she had set up for me were either with someone who was looking for a second wife to bare his child, or a traveling salesman from another state who was looking for a mistress to have companionship while he was in town. My mother said that since I am a "damaged woman" I should take the offer, because I would never find anyone else better than them. I am sure that in her own mind she was only trying to look out for my best interest, but I can't help but think that she was just trying to get me out of her sight. With my mother's dismay I refused both offers, left my parents' home and went to the city called Yongsan, next to the capital city of Seoul.

Chapter Five

In the big city, I found out that there
were many job brokers. You would check
in with the receptionist and sit in the
lobby until someone came along and
decided to hire you for whatever work
that might be available. Of course, these
jobs were not office clerks, or any other
prestigious job but more like jobs for the
uneducated. The jobs they offered were
things like a coffee/tea house hostess,
cocktail waitress or kisaeng, which is
similar to a Geisha girl in Japan. Being a
woman without an education and no
good work history, you would be lucky to
even be hired for any of those jobs. I sat in
the lobby where several women waited to
be hired just like me. Almost a half day
later, my name was called and I met with
a woman who was offering a job as a
coffee/tea house hostess which came
with room and board. Requirements for
being a hostess at the coffee/tea house
included being mature, pretty and poised,

to draw customers attention. There are
many different levels of coffee/tea houses
in Korea. There are places for mature
customers which are mostly for business
meetings and then there are places for
college students or places for just
everyday ordinary forks. These places are
not for just drinking tea or coffee,
although people do enjoy a good cup of
coffee or tea; but serve as meeting places
for lovers, friends and sometimes to
discuss their businesses.

The coffee/tea houses served a
variety of herbal teas (some are very
expensive) and you could also have a
shot of whiskey in your coffee or tea. The
music is a big part of the tea house and
they must have a DJ. The choice of music
needs to be suitable for the populations
they serve. In college towns, students
gathered to mingle with friends, meet
girls or boys and request their favorite
pop songs to DJ. The hostess plays a very
important role in this business, especially
where the mature population gathers.
The hostess usually dressed in colorful

Korean custom dress and her hair must
be in an 'up-do'; the hostess also needed
to memorize customers by their last
names, greet them and make sure that
the frequent visitors are welcomed and
honored. I took the job at the first offer,
because I knew another opportunity may
not come again for a long time, and I also
needed the place to stay.

The coffee/tea house I was hired at
was located in one of the busiest business
district and customers were mostly
middle-aged men. The first day at the job,
I wore a satin white Korean custom dress,
trimmed with rainbow color fabric. I had
my hair done at the salon and pinned up
with a pearl inlaid clip. I was nervous,
because I have never worked in a place
where I was the center of attention.
Somehow, many customers enjoyed my
tamed mannerism and my youthful fresh
looks. The lodging that was offered by the
tea shop owner was small and shared
with two or three waitresses, and the
owner provided us with one meal per
day, which was a bowl of rice and kimchi.

Although this job sounds glamorous, the pay was little and most of my pay went to new clothes and weekly salon visits to keep up with my appearance. I kept contact with my mother and sent money to her whenever I could. Life in the fast lane kept me busy, but there was a lingering sadness and a huge hole in my heart, and a hunger that I could not fulfill with anything that I was doing at the coffee/tea house. I missed my kids. I missed them so terribly; I cried myself to sleep at night, wondering how they were doing, wondering if they were crying for me, and if they were being loved and cared for. I thought that if I had the chance to live only one day with my kids, I would gladly give up my life.

The harboring of empty unsettled feelings and insecurity made me move from job to job in different towns. I was searching endlessly for something to fill my emptiness and mend my broken heart. A year had gone by since I left my hometown, and I ended up in an upscale traditional saloon calls Yojoung, as a one

of Kisaeng (which is similar to Geisha girl
in Japan). The place I worked was
spacious and fully staffed with chefs and
house keepers. There were many kisaeng
to host private and group parties. The
food and drink they served was
traditional Korean food, equivalent to the
meals served for royal family. Kisaengs
are not allowed to eat this food because
we are not there to eat, but to entertain.
Many well-known businessmen had their
monthly gatherings and business
meetings at this saloon, and sometimes
politicians came to have their political
discussions.

Being a kisaeng required you to
have some sort of talents, like folk
singing, folk dancing or play traditional
musical instruments. Few are hired for
just their beauty and those folks were
called an 'exotic kisaeng'. They wore old
traditional dresses that are colorful and
adorned with expensive ornaments in
front of their dresses and on their pinned-
up hair. She was usually the last woman
to enter the room while men waited in

anticipation to gaze at her beauty, hoping
she would set next to/assist them.
Kisaeng are not there to engage in any
sexual relationship as most people
imagine, but they are entertainers with
musical instruments, dancers and singers
of traditional songs. Some of the kisaengs
are intelligent enough to have knowledge
in politics and engage in conversations.
Even so, sometimes men could be cruel
and slap women on the face for dozing
off, because these parties could go on
until the early morning. The privileged
Kisaengs lived in a house where they
worked, two meals were provided by
chefs, and rooms were cleaned by house
keepers. Kisaengs are responsible for
their own laundry and take care of
themselves to stay healthy and desirable,
intellectually and in their physical
appearance.

I was one of the popular ones
among customers, the owner of the house
respected me and I was liked by other
girls. However, my emotions were
unsteady, which prohibited me from

getting close to anyone and I moved one place to another often. I became ill, and could not eat or sleep and I had no energy to get up and apply myself to work, and I missed my kids more and more every day. I felt as though I was not going to be able to sustain myself if I didn't see them at least once, and know that they were doing well. I finally asked permission from the owner for a three days' vacation and got on the train headed back to the Inchon city. When I arrived at the station, I used a pay phone to contact the children's father at his work and asked him if I could meet with him. I remembered it like it was yesterday, I sat in the cafe near his work and waited for him impatiently. When I saw him walking through the entrance, I felt like I was choking with tears, but he showed no emotions. He was just as cold as the day he forced me to divorce him.

I composed myself, and let him know that I came to ask if I could have permission to see kids...but before I had finished the sentence he responded in a

firm tone "that is not possible". I begged
him as I was sobbing to just let me see
them for one last time. I told him that it's
okay if it was even from a distance, that
than I would be okay and would not
bother him ever again. He stood up from
the chair, put out his cigarette in the ash
tray and said "I am sorry, but it is too late
for that". I cannot let you see them,
because they already have forgotten
about you; please don't contact me
again". I started to weep like a child, I
knelt down on the floor and begged, but
he threw some change for the tea he had
ordered and briskly walked out the door.
The pain I felt on my chest was even
more painful than the time I fell to the
asphalt from jumping off the bridge.

After a long while I was able to
regroup myself, and walked out of the
cafe feeling everyone's eyes on back of
my head. Since I was in Inchon, I decided
to visit my parents before I returned to
my job in Yongsan. My parents were glad
to see me and they appeared to be doing
okay. I was happy to hear that my brother

and sisters were working and doing as
well. At night while everyone was asleep,
I told mother that the reason for visiting
Inchon was that I was hoping to see my
kids, but I was denied. My mother then
advised me to move on with my own life.
She said that a few weeks ago she went to
my ex-husband's home town, and hung
around nearby to see if she could get a
glimpse of her grandson (after all she was
the one who helped deliver him). She said
that by mid-afternoon, she saw my son
Jinsuk walking into the convenience
store. She called out his name and he
came over to see her. She asked him if he
remembered her and he replied "yes, you
are my other grandmother". She asked
him "Where is your father?" and he
replied "he is taking a nap with my mom
and the baby". She asked "your mom?"
and he replied "yes, I have a step mom
and I have a baby sister....dad said that
my real mom is dead.... she is buried next
to my grandpa in the cemetery.We just
visited them couple of days ago".
Listening to my mother's story, I felt like
my heart had stopped for a second and I
could not breathe. I got dizzy and felt like

vomiting. I left my parent's home that evening in despair; I felt empty and hollow and I promised myself I wouldn't be coming back to Incheon again, and I would not look for them again for their own sake. On my way back to Yongsan, I stopped at the Buddhist temple, made an offering and said a prayer for the well-being of my two children and also for their family. I want their family to do well so my children can be well cared for.

After returning to Yojoung, I became a different person. I began to smoke and often drank until I passed out. Once I went out on a date with a customer and ended up climbing out of the bathroom window and left my date waiting in the room. I met a man who I began dating, and told him that I was the oldest daughter of 5 girls to a wealthy business man. On our first date I took all 4 girls from my work and introduced them as they were my younger sisters and made him pay for their lunch. I did this for every date with him, and the girls enjoyed free food and watched me play pranks on this guy.

When things got complicate, I simply moved to another town and start all over again. However, the people in some places were not as nice as other places. The owner at the new Yojoung were not pleased with me and the girls there were not friendly with me as other girls had been in the past. One evening we were hosting a party and I came down with a terrible headache and had abdominal pain because I was having a heavy period. The madam noticed that I wasn't at my best and she got upset with me. She called me out of the party room and yelled at me for not paying attention to customers. I told her that I needed to excuse myself for the night, because I was not feeling well. She replied "this is your last day and I want you to be out of the house by morning, you understand me!?...'If you think you going to get away with everything, because you got a pretty little face, you got another thing coming!". Regardless of what she said about me, I

didn't feel like arguing with her so I went
to the bedroom (shared with other girls)
to rest. The room was dark and no one
was there because all other girls were
hosting a big party in the main hall. I lay
on the floor, pulled up the blanket and
covered my face as a million things ran
through my mind. Suddenly, I heard a
noise and saw a shadow of a person at the
bedroom door.

The door was a simple sliding door
trimmed with thin wood and covered
with the rice paper. The lock on the door
was a little hook that could easily lift
with any thin object. I sat up as I
watched the door lock lifting and slowly
pushing to the side. It must have been
one of the men from the party but it was
too dark to see who it was. He walked in
slowly, put his finger across his mouth
and hand motioned to me not to make
any noise. He already had taken off his
jacket and dress shirt, and I could see his
white t-shirt and the dark pants. I sat up
and pulled the blanket up to my chin and
pleaded with him not to come near me,

but he quickly landed on top of me. I started to cry and tried to push him away as I told him that I was having a heavy period and that I had abdominal pain, but he covered my mouth with one hand and raped me anyway. I was gasping for air and I am sure that someone from outside of the room heard me struggling, but no one came to my rescue. When the man finished, he stooped down and whispered to my ear "I am coming back for you". I was disgusted at myself.

While everyone was asleep, I went outside where the water pump was and washed myself with the cold water and threw my soiled stuff into the pile of trash. That morning before the dawn, I packed my suitcase and left the place without saying goodbye to anyone. You may wonder why I didn't I tell anyone what happened; because no one cared, I would just be humiliated and ridiculed. It was easier to just let it go and act as nothing ever happened.

Another summer had gone by without having any meaning to life except that I was still breathing and working at another place in another town. It was a warm sunny afternoon and I sat at the table in the far corner of my favorite coffee/tea house. I went there often for a cup of hot coffee and request a few songs that I enjoyed. My preference of music was the classical style, but I also liked to listen to Tom Jones (Green Green Grass of home) and the "Song Sung Blue" by Neil Diamond. I didn't understand the English lyrics but I liked the sound of music. Sometimes I closed my eyes and listened to the classical music that someone requested to DJ. When the music ended, I opened my eyes and there was a young girl with long hair who sat across the table from me where I was sitting. She said "I hope you don't mind, you see, all other tables are full" and she added "it's busy place ha?" I told her that it is usually busy this time of the day and I didn't mind sharing the table with her; besides, I could use some company. When the waitress came for an order, she ordered a cup of hot coffee with the shot of whiskey. I was surprised, because she seemed to be modest person and did not appear to be the kind of girl who would drink liquor, especially in the bright daylight.

After watching her drink about three cups of coffee, all with the shot of whiskey, I asked her kindly "are you alright? you seem as though something is troubling you" She than replied "my name is Sujin, it's nice to meet you". She said that she was from the countryside where she lived with her widowed father. She said that her parents owned a large farm where they grew grains and beans, but her mother passed away 3 years ago from stomach cancer. She said that she came to Seoul to visit with her fiancée who attends the university there. She found out that her fiancée met someone who attends the same school and he announced that he was breaking off the engagement with her. Sujin was tearful as she shared her story and I felt sympathetic toward her. Sujin also said that she does not want to disappoint her father by returning home too soon and would like to spend some time exploring the city. She asked me if I could show her around, because she had never been to a big city before. I spent the next 3 days showing her around; I took her to museums, shopping centers, had lunch and saw a movie with her. She thanked me for my hospitality and said that she would be going back to her home the next day and she asked me if I could come with her. She said "my father will be delighted to meet you" and added "it is so beautiful this time of the year". Please, come with me, why don't you take a little vacation for yourself. I promise I won't make you do any harvest work" and she chuckled. She seemed harmless and I thought to myself that having a mini vacation didn't sound too bad.

The next day, late afternoon I was on the bus with Sujin headed out to see the countryside, hoping to breathe some fresh air, watch the blue sky and enjoy the harvest season. By the time we got off from the bus and the train, it was already at dark. She then said that she needed to stop at the cafe where she worked part time, which she never mentioned to me before. She said that she needed to let her boss know that she was back, so she could set up the work schedule for the following week. She stopped a cab and said "hop in, it's not walking distance". The cab driver lit his cigarette and started to smoke as he drove through the bumpy dirt road and lastly came to a small village. I thought it was odd to see neon signs, and it seemed busy for the little town. The taxi driver pulled up behind the large building, dropped us off, took the fare money and drove off. Sujin walked behind me as we proceeded through the back door. She insisted that I should meet her boss because she is the nicest person I would ever meet and she would be happy to meet someone from the city. I felt a little offbeat but I brushed off the uneasy feeling and walked into the heavy back door as Sujin hurried me. When we entered the door there was a guy with heavy muscles who locked the door behind us and led us through the narrow passage.

Sujin explained that the back entrance was for the employees and he is there for security purposes. As we entered through the narrow passage, we were happily greeted by a middle-aged woman with a gold tooth that showed when she smiled. In those days having gold teeth was not uncommon. It is to show that you have money and the merit of beauty. She seemed to be kind and led us through the hallway with little rooms in a row as she exclaimed to Sujin "you brought the good one this time!" Sujin then responded as she disappeared through the hallway "I told you I would". The woman responded "good job girl, I know I have faith in you" As we walked further into the place I kept hearing loud music in the background. It sounded like it was coming from the café, though it seemed a little too loud for a cafe. The woman who greeted me also disappeared down the hallway and I was left in the room with the security guard who stood at the corner, with his arms crossed on his chest. "Excuse me where is the bathroom?" I asked. The man replied "you need stay put until madam comes back!" the man replied with authoritarian manner. "What is this place? Where is Sujin?" I asked with a trembling voice. The man stood by the door remained silent, took out a cigarette, put it in corner of his mouth, lit it, and puff out smoke, staring at me with a smirk on his face. The door to the front hallway was cracked open and I could see people, young and old alike, walking by like they did not see me. One older woman peeked into the room, holding cigarette between two fingers and cracked a smile at me but she quickly disappeared. She looked as though she was in her 40's and I could see that she had an ugly scar on her cheek that pulled the corner of her mouth when she smiled.

Something was telling me that I was in some kind of trouble but I couldn't get anyone to talk. I bolted upright from the chair and shout out "I need to go to the bathroom and I need to talk to Sujin! Where is she?!" Suddenly, the man rushed over to me, grabbed my shoulder and thrust me down to the chair. He held down my neck to the table and I bit my lips from the force and bled. He shouted "I said sit down! and shut the f..k up!" then he said "oh dear god have mercy, are you really that stupid??!!You are now madam's property and you are not going anywhere, you numb skull!" My eyes felt heavy with swollen and blurred from crying. The clock on the dining area wall showed well passed 2:00 in the morning. I heard the woman who greeted me at the back entrance come into the room and sit in front of me. "You will sleep in our room with me and my husband tonight". We will discuss things in the morning, because I am exhausted and need to get some sleep". I begged her "Ma'am, I need to go back to the city, please let me go, I won't tell anyone just let me go". I pleaded but she just chuckled and said "don't worry honey, you are going to be just fine here, I'll talk to you in the morning". I realized that me getting out of there was not going to happen. Just as she said, I had to stay in their room with her, her husband and their daughter. Their little girl looked about 4-5 months old and they all slept on one side of the room and I stay on the far side in fetal position and cried. The couple did not seem to be mean people, but it is unacceptable and a lousy way to get rich by selling other people's bodies, especially when they have a little girl of their own. .

Their morning started really late and the owner (couple) of the cafe, or rather 'pimps' finally sat with me close to lunch hour. I began to panic and cried hysterically. What madam was saying sounded like Sujin was a human trafficker, who borrowed money from madam when she needed and repaid her with bringing in young girls. I told her that I am not a young girl and I had given birth to 2 children and they would have no use for me. She laughed at my plea and said that in order for me to leave, I had to pay her back what she gave Sujin, with interests and of course, what I had in my pocket book was just small change.

The couple got extremely upset at my opposition, and the husband slapped my face saying "who the hell you think you are ha?" Then the madam said "oh honey don't hit her, we don't want our good merchandise to be damaged we will just lock her up until she comes to her senses". Madam ordered the guard to lock me in one of the small rooms yelling "watch out for her!" The guard grabbed me by the arm and also a handful of my hair, dragged me and pushed me into the room. "You better lighten up if you know what's good for you!!" he said, and as he turned around, I could hear him grumbling "what a stupid bitch". In the room there was a little pot in the corner for me to use as portable toilet. I refused to eat or drink and a few days later the madam came in and said "I tell you what, I will train you for bartender and you will work behind the counter and we'll see what happens from there" than she added "you are damn lucky I like you, otherwise I could just hand you over to someone who likes hurting girls"... and it could be lot worse than dying." What could be worse than dying I thought? That comment actually put chills through my bones.

     The place I was captured was a small village not too far from city called "Dongducheon" where the Camp Casey U.S. military was located. I was resentful for being there and blamed myself for being so gullible after all I went through; but on the other hand, I was glad to work behind the counter instead of working as what they called "a yankee whore". "During and following the Korean war, prostitutes in South Korea were frequently used by the U.S. military. Prostitutes servicing members of the U.S. military in South Korea have been known locally under a variety of terms. At the beginning they used term Yankee princess is a common name and literal meaning for the prostitutes in the "Gijichon", U.S. military Camp Towns in South Korea. Yankee whore or Yanggalbo and Western whore are also common names. On the other hand, it is also used as an insulting epithet. Until the early

1990s, the term Wianbu another word as "Comfort Women" was often used by South Korean media and officials to refer to prostitutes for U.S. military, but comfort women was also the euphemism used for the sex slaves for the Imperial Japanese Army and in order to avoid confusions, the term "Yanggongju" replaced Wianbu to refer to sexual laborers for the U.S. military". (From Wikipedia, the free encyclopedia February 2017)

The madam provided me with a new outfit, shoes and toiletries, again all added to my debt, on top of the food and lodging...not to mention the principal and the rising interest from the time Sujin sold me. The security man always stood beside me even at the bar counter, making sure that I am doing my job. My sleeping quarters were with several girls whom have been there for a while. One of the girls said that "it does not matter how many times you open your legs, you will never make enough money to pay off your debt". "They will let you go when

you are no longer useful, it means when
you are old, so good luck to you".

Before I go on with my story in
military village, I should explain more
about the culture of these brothels during
this time in Korea. There was no birth
control plan for girls. We were taught to
take care of ourselves, such as washing
private parts with the toothpaste after
having sex. If one does get pregnant, she
would be sent to the clinic outside of the
village to get an abortion and her debt
will go up according to the cost of
abortion. She would not only owe the cost
of the abortion but during the week of
recovery, you can't make any money so
the debt goes up even more. I had no idea
back then, but later I found out that these
kinds of operations were supported and
protected by both Korean and American
government.

These kinds of operations were in
every village where the American
military bases existed. Sure, there are

women who chose to do what they do to support their family. Some are working to send their siblings for a higher education, or paying for treatment costs for family members who are ill and the list goes on. Even so, I can assure you that no one is there because they enjoy having sex multiple times a day with men they don't like and be treated like waste. However, at least 65% of prostitutes in that village were at one point, either coerced, kidnapped or even sold by their own family members for money.

All prostitutes in the village were equipped with a medical booklet which was issued by the Korean government and each time you pass the test, they will mark with the stamp. The MP (American military police) would go around the village and raid the night clubs twice a week to make sure that women are up to date with their check-ups and VD shots on their little brown booklets. Sure, there was a written law prohibiting American soldiers to engage in any human trafficking and prostitution, but it was just a piece of paper hanging on the wall. Nobody is there to enforce the law or prohibit them from engaging in such acts, neither the Korean government, law enforcement or American military force...rather, they protected the brothel owners. There was an article under the Politico edition, in which it was written "The problems associated with the sex trade are particularly pronounced in South Korea, where "camp towns" that surrounded U.S. bases have become deeply entrenched in the country's economy, politics and culture. Dating back to the 1945 U.S occupation of Korea, when GIs casually bought sex with as little as a cost of cigarette, and these camp-towns have been the center of an exploitative and profoundly disturbing sex industry and it became deeply stigmatized twilight zones. One that both displays and reinforces the military's attitudes about men, women, power and dominance. No one talked about the problems existed in those days but we all knew that the Korean government actually established the sex business industry, using helpless women to earn

American dollars in order to relieve national debts. Yet, when women are no longer useful due age or illness, they dismiss them like they never existed, because recognition means they are admitting their wrong doing. Later I found out that the village I got locked up in was called 'Songsan' which is not far from Camp Casey, the home of the 2nd Infantry Division, US Army. The camp is located in Tongduchon, Korea, approximately forty miles North of Seoul, and 11 miles south of the Demilitarized Zone. It was not that far from Youngsan where I was working and resided, but somehow I never knew that this place existed because it was a totally different world. Women's sex work had long been used to help keep male troops happy or at least happy enough to keep working for the military. Also, in the village there was a clinic (which was a small room with a little bed, similar to the bed in the abortion clinic) to check on women for STD and they sent us there like cattle to a barn. We would be waiting in line, panic stricken, wondering if we were going to pass the examination.

If any girl failed her check-ups,
she'd be taken away by M.P. to the
American military base, like a criminal,
and into the building known as the
"monkey house" but the truth was it was
a jail/clinic. The women who were taken
to the base would be forced to receive
heavy doses of penicillin, which often, the
potency of the medicine alone would kill
underage girls. The girl who witnessed
the scene described that a girl who got a
heavy dose would fall to the cement floor
having convulsions, with white foam
coming out of her mouth, and then stop
breathing. Girls who died at the clinic did
not get proper burials, but were buried
anonymously in the abandoned field
behind the base with numbers written on
a stick as a marker; there were hundreds
of them. There was no investigation or
notification to their family when girls
died inside the clinic, families were just
told they "left the town". They were no
follow up necessary, and people
eventually forgot about them as they ever
existed.

These girls didn't just die from
sickness or mismanaged drug overdoses,
but many of them were murdered by
soldiers from unimaginable sexual abuse.
There was a time that a soldier shot both
his girlfriend and their child because he
did not want to be responsible for their
welfare. I was also astounded to hear the
news about a young woman who was
murdered in 1992, in the same village I
was captured in in the 1970's. The news
was all over Korea, about the young man
name K. Markle. who served in the U.S.
army as a medic at Camp Casey; the same
base as Tom and Randy were. This was
the most gruesome murder ever
committed by a U. S soldier in Korea,
after the time that the army tank willfully
ran-over two Jr. high school girls while
walking to their friend's house. The
soldier thought it was funny, chasing
them with the tank while they were
frenetically running as they tried to avoid
the tank, until they were ultimately run
over. These innocent girls were killed at

the hands of a soldier being drunk and ignorant.

Nevertheless, K. Markle murdered a young woman who lived in a village outside of Camp Casey. Her body was founded beaten; he hit her with a bottle on her face and her head, and she was found with an umbrella in her anus, a coke bottle in her vagina, and laundry detergent spread all over her bloody body. This incident angered both the Korean community and American militaries. Kenneth was indicted but he only received a minimum sentence. The incident occurred 16 years after I came to the states and yet, it disturbed me enough to have nightmares. But who is to blame? The Korean government treated women like waste and lay down our lives to save their country's economy. Still, they discarded these women when they could no longer be useful. How can you expect others to treat us any better? Many Koreans in those days or even now, they treated us like human waste. Sadly, even nowadays in America, people who have immigrated to this country because one of their family members married to American man, are ashamed to acknowledge her as family and often turn their face from them. Some may put on a good face in front of us, but when they turn around still call us "Yankee whore". When I came to the U.S, I found it extremely difficult to blend in to Korean society in the U.S., especially as a person like me who has had a failed marriage with an American man. On top of that, it felt like if you were not living in a big house, and driving fancy cars, then you are simply a "loser" and people will look down at you as "less than" they are. These acts are especially prevalent in Korean churches with people who profess them as Christians. No one likes to speak the truth and most of them are "just go with the flow".

Chapter Six

Back to my story... in the brothel, bar
tendering was not hard as I thought,
because there were no fancy drinks that
were sold, and once I learned simple
tricks to make mixed drinks it became
easy. The cigarette smoke filled the club
at night and the room would be packed
with GIs looking to see who they could
chose for quick pleasure or to spend the
night with. Some are there to just drink,
dance and have fun. The loud western
music shook the club, while a disco ball
hung from the ceiling spun around with
the twinkling lights. Girls with tight mini-
skirts or bell bottom pants with halter
tops and platform heels danced under the
flashing lights, many of them were under
the influences of marijuana we called
"happy smoke" or alcohol to forget the
reality. Soon, I began to notice that there
was a handsome young soldier name Tom
who came to the club just about every
night; he always sat at the corner of the
bar and ordered coca cola. He would sit
for hours with one hand on the cola glass

and his other hand under his chin with his elbow on the counter. He often stared at me until he returned to the barracks before the curfew was called at 11:00pm. He never made a move or said anything to me, but just smiled. Many girls tried to attract him but he wouldn't budge.

As the time passed, several GIs got curious about me and start to place bids with the madam. Eventually I was sold to the highest bidder for one month. Madam said "I like you but I am in it for the business and you are no exception". I simply gave up fighting, because I felt like there's no use because it was going to happen sooner or later; besides I thought that I may get one step closer to paying off my debt. There I was, sold to a chubby looking GI as a sex partner for the entire month. Madam said that she sold me for $150.00 but I still had an outstanding balance, because now she provided me with the private room and the bed. No sense in arguing because I knew I wasn't going anywhere. The GI I was sold to had no real interest in me, except use me as a sexual object. I don't think he even cared to know who I was as a human being. After the long and humiliating month was finally over and I expected to go back to serving drinks at the bar, but I couldn't have been more wrong.

I was told by the madam that I wouldn't be working at the bar again, because now I was "broken in"..... "you are going to work with other girls" she said, and then she advised the rules I should keep in mind. "Always get paid first, bring the money to me, then you do your business". The price for serving a GI was $5.00 for short time and $15.00 for the overnight. I did not know what else I could do to save myself from falling further into this 'abyss'. That night I wept and prayed to God please, please take me.... I pity myself..... I hate myself.... please, put me to sleep and never to wake me up........

Hours passed and I heard the knock on the door. I regrouped myself and open the door to find one of the other girls

Autobiography by Un Chu Lee-
Hoyle

standing in door way. She said "Hey Tom is looking for you out at the club". I was surprised and walked out to the club and Tom was sitting at the bar with a concerned look. He said that he heard me crying and asked girls what's going on with "Mini", which was my nick name. He also said that he found out what was about to happen and he wanted to help me. He then took me to madam and asked her how much my debt was. He also asked her if she would give him two weeks to get the money to pay off my debt. She was astounded by his request, responding "what are you? Some kind of crazy? Really? Why? The price for setting her free is $850.00...with that kind of money, you can have any girl you want, but if you really want her bring the money, then she is all yours!" Can you imagine people are being forced to sell their body for the rest of their life because of a measly $850.00? It was what it was and nevertheless, $850.00 was lot of money for us compared to the prices they charged for selling sex. Tom replied "Okay, no problem, I will be back in two weeks with the money and you

145

promise, you will let her go!" She laughed at him and said "two weeks Tom, not a day later and if you don't show up, she is going to start work and that's a promise!"

Exactly on the 14th day, as he promised, I saw Tom hurrying through the front door; he grabbed my hand and walked straight to the madam's room. He pulled out a bundle of cash from his sweatshirt pocket "Here it is all there, she is free to go right?!" Tom proudly said. "Wow Tom, you are one crazy son of bitch!" she said as she counted money. "Okay she is all yours, oh my goodness". My mouth was dried and my heart was racing, like the coal train pumping off smoke with its wheels racing through the track. I prayed that this was not a dream, and if it was "Please, please don't wake me up" I thought. The madam exclaimed "You are one lucky girl, I have never seen anything like this before in my life; now you go ahead and have a good life!"

Tom was young, handsome with blue
eyes and light brown hair with curls;
people said that he looks just like the
movie star from the "Love Story". I do
agree he had a strong resemblance to
young Ryan O'Neill and that face is only
way I can remember him. Tom was
sweet, generous and did not expect
anything in return. Tom came to pick me
up the next day and we went to look for a
rental place in the village. It was easy to
rent a place in camp-town if you have the
money up front, and there was no credit
check or references. Tom paid for the
rent and gave me enough money to buy
necessary items like pots, pans, dishes
and groceries. In was the first time in
years I was sleeping in my own room and
I was so happy. The following month Tom
even bought me a black and white
console TV and I was ever so proud. Tom
and I started to date like normal people
and we held hands in public like a couple.
Tom treated with me with respect; he
was gentle, kind, consistent with his word
and had a great sense of humor, which
made me laugh. Even though I didn't
speak his language (except some broken

English), we were able to communicate
with gestures and he respond to me with
broken English so I can understand and
learn more.

   We used to go hiking on
the mountains and soak our feet
in cool streams by the waterfall.
He would take off his jacket and
lay it on the grass for me to sit
and tell me about his family. As I
said I spoke very little broken
English, but I could understand a
lot of what he was talking about.
He told me that his sister had a
beauty salon in their hometown,
which I believe was somewhere
in Minnesota. She had a fish tank
in her shop with many 'guppies'
because they were always
"having babies" and he laughed.
He showed me a photo of him
and his brothers and cousins
standing around the 18 wheelers
truck with a beer company logo.
He talked about his German
grandmother who was stubborn

just like my grandmother. I was
falling in love with him...but I
knew very well that this was not
going to last forever, because he
would have to return to the
States when his assignment was
over in Korea. Tom wanted to
marry me, but he was only 19
years old and needed his
parent's consent as well as
required approval from the U.S
military.

One day we took a trip to
Yougsan Garrison, which is an
area that served as the
headquarters for U.S. military
forces stationed in South Korea,
known as United States Forces
Korea (USFK). It is the place
known for United States Army
Garrison Yougsan (USAG-
Yougsan) under the supervision
of the installation Management
Command Pacific Region. This
place once served as
headquarters for the Imperial

Japanese Army during World
War II while Japanese occupied
Korea from 1910 to 1945.
However, Tom was able to sign
me in to the base where he could
make phone calls to his parents
in the state. When he called his
parents and explained the
situation and asked for consent,
they were troubled. His parents
told him that it was against their
Catholic belief, marriage to a
foreign woman who was also
older than their son. They had a
long history of faith in their
Catholic religion and my
circumstance was not exactly in
their favor. Tom disputed with
his parents and told them that
he would not return to the States
without me. He also told his
parents that he would re-enlist
his service in Korea till he
reached 21.

About a month after Tom made the
call to his parents, he received a letter

from them pleading for him to return home. They gave him permission for our engagement, along with a gold bracelet for me as a token of acceptance. Tom asked his parents to sell his car and send money to him, so we could start working on my visa. However, getting a visa, especially without being married was a long process and I had to take many trips to Seoul. The man I hired, who was supposedly an expert on the visa process, was not helpful but I didn't have the smarts to know any better and he took advantage of my situation. I had no idea of the status for my visa; I got a passport and rest of the money was drained, and Tom's parents demanded him to return home. I know now that most of this happened, because, I was uneducated and had no street smarts. That being said, one night we had an argument about not getting the paperwork done on time and Tom stormed out of the apartment. I thought he was just upset and would be back the next day but I did not hear from him. Almost a week went gone by without hearing from him and I began to worry. I went out to look for him and found a couple of guys from Tom's barracks, who informed me that he left Korea to return home in America..... He left without saying goodbye.

I was utterly alone in the room... I couldn't breathe, I felt like my heart dropped to the deepest pit and felt like my entire body was empty like a ghost. I missed him.....he didn't say good bye... I stayed awake night after night, hoping that he would walk through the door and hold me. The time went by so slow, endless nights and days had past and I came to the realization that he was not coming back. "He probably forgot all about me...." I thought. Once again, I sought to die. It was winter and I had a coal stove in the center of my room for heat. This particular coal emitted strong carbon monoxide, which could easily kill a room full of people if the cover was left open, especially with a fresh block of coal. One evening I locked my door, removed the metal lid from the stove, placed a fresh block of coal in, and I fell into a deep sleep. Fortunately, or unfortunately, one

of the girls from the village was passing
by and noticed the foul order coming
from my room, and she called for help and
broke the door open. When they found
me, I was unconscious and soaked in my
own urine. When I woke up in my room, I
didn't remember going to the hospital or
coming home. I found myself laying on the
floor with a loss of hearing, sense of smell
and blurred vision which lasted for
months after waking up from
unconsciousness...but here again I am,
alive....

One night I dreamt that someone
who was very tall was standing beside
my bed with a white sheet over his head.
The frightening dream woke me, and I
sat up at the edge of the bed. Suddenly I
heard something loud like a thunder
sound, followed by the sound of pouring
rain. I looked out the window, but I didn't
see any rain; I kept hearing strange
noises on the roof top. It was the dead of
winter and I put my coat over the night
gown and stepped outside to see what
was going on. I looked up and saw smoke

coming from the roof. I walked around the building and saw a ball of fire spewing out of the home next door. The village was in a remote place and there was no fire station. I screamed out to the village "Fire...!!!". The shouting woke up the village people and men came with buckets of water, kicked down the burning door and tried to put out the fire, but it was almost impossible. I could not go back to my room because the roof was engulfed with flames and blowing over to my side of the apartment. I knelt on the icy ground and called God again in desperation. Amazingly, the wind began to blow the other way, and the village people were able to put out the fire before it consumed my room with all that I had.

I thought about leaving the village and starting over, but there was a part of me that wanted to believe that one day Tom would come back and look for me. There was no one to hold me back, but I became a hostage of my own self. I also forgot to mention that my mother faithfully visited every month to collect her allowance since Tom set me free from madam's hand. When Tom rescued me, I went to visit my family; it had been 2 years since I had gone missing. My parents thought I was dead. Since I reunited with my parents, mother started to visit me and mentioned our family's financial problems. I felt sorry for my family, and helped my mother out, which naturally became my responsibility. I would save money each month, tucked away inside a sock and place it under the drawer for my mother to collect. When she came, I usually ordered her favorite Chinese dish for her to eat before leaving. One day she complained "Why are you always ordering same dish, I am tired of eating the same food, can't you order something else?" I was in my mid 20's, free from sex slavery and I could go anywhere and do anything, but I chose to stay in the village, hoping that someday Tom would return and look for me. Besides, I thought, where am I going to go? I was too damaged, psychologically and physically. Some may say that no one would know me if I moved far away enough, and I didn't have to tell anyone my life story... It is true, but I can't turn off my emotions and I know who I am. I felt as though I was nothing more than "TRASH".

The life in the village where brothels was not a pleasant place to be. The majority of people are mean and harsh to women like me. They called us names, such as "Yankee whore" and some people even spit at you when walking by. Some Korean men will look at you and makes humping gestures while laughing and spitting. Now, my only dream was to escape from Korea and go to America, the land of freedom where women are free of abuse and men will respect women...at least that's what I thought. When the evenings would come, I stood by the front gate of the military compound with other girls. I was 5 feet tall, weighted 90-95 pounds with the long black hair; I usually wore a dress shirt, bell bottom pants and platform sandals. I never dressed seductively or

showed cleavage, yet, GIs found me
attractive and some of them were kind.

The bus from the officer's club on
the military base would drive up to the
gate and once we all got on, the bus
would drive back to the base and let us
off in front of the officer's club. There
would be music, drinks and both army
officers looking to dance with girls as
well as some officers there with their
wives. Some of military wives chose to
live in Korea to be with their husbands,
and I don't remember any of those
women being prejudiced against us. I've
met quite a few nice soldiers, but their
interests were not on me as a human
being but just as sex objects. Can I blame
them? Of course not, because that is how
our country, the Korean government
portrayed us, as "sex object" and how can
I expect others to treat us any better.

There was a beautiful young girl
who met a soldier, got engaged and had a
beautiful son. She had a nice place to live

and had a nanny to care for her baby, and she was the envy of many women in the village. She seemed so happy, and she was generous and kind to others. However, one day she disappeared out of thin air. The last time someone saw her was when she was hiking up to the mountains with her fiancé. A few weeks had gone by but she did not come home, and the nanny started to worry and contacted her family. Then the nanny started to have dreams about the baby's mother. The nanny said that she came into her dreams and begged the nanny to find her. She would say that she was on the mountain beneath the rock, cold, hungry and scared. After having the same dream for several nights, the nanny went to the local police and pleaded with them to look for her. The search began with people in the village, mostly "camp-town women". When their search was unsuccessful, the women began to rally in front of the military base. The nanny contacted the girl's parents and soon the family members arrived, including the girl's mother, who sat out in front of the military base day after day. The Korean police finally started to pay attention, and began a search with the help of the American military. From the village, people could see the lower mountain covered with people who were searching for the baby's mother. Unfortunately, a couple of weeks into the search a group of young boys found the girl's corpse, buried underneath rocks on the side of the mountain.

After they located her body many people went up to the mountain and I joined in. When we got up to the mountain the police were placing her body on to the stretcher. I saw her partially decomposed blackish body, with skull half gone from being hit with the rocks. A couple of witnesses came forward and told Korean police, as well as the military police that they witnessed her hiking up to the mountain with her fiancé the night before her disappearance. Her fiancé was questioned, and eventually he admitted that he killed her because he wanted to take his son back to the U.S., but she was not willing to give him up. He further admitted that he had no plan to take her to U.S. but he wanted his child. He also said that he buried her with rocks according to his Native American tradition and therefore he had done nothing wrong. The people from the village fought for him to be persecuted in Korea but he was sent back to U.S. and there was no follow up. I believe the child was given to a Korean family and later he was adopted by an American family in the U.S. There were many half-bred or mixed children in the village back in the days. Some were lucky enough to get adopted by American families from the states, but many who were left behind suffered a great deal of racism, especially for half black children. The mixed children were not welcomed in schools or accepted in Korean society. They got teased, bullied and ostracized t and most of them lived life in misery.

In spite of all that happened, my long-waited wishes ultimately came true. One afternoon, a couple of Tom's old friends delivered a letter from him! I was ecstatic, but I didn't know how to read or write English. I took the letter to the interpreter in the village, who read to me- "I regret that I left without saying goodbye to you. My time was up and your visa was not ready and I didn't have the heart to tell you that I had to leave". He said that he had been sick and he been in and out of hospitals, but he wants to try to send for me. His friend who delivered the letter, hand-motioned using his index finger, and pointed to side of his head in circling motion. That made me think maybe he was trying to tell me that Tom was in and out of psychiatric care. I tried to send a letter back to Tom, but I was not sure that my corresponding letter I sent ever got to him, because I never heard from him again. The interpreter moved away and he took Tom's address with him and never saw him again. Tom's last name was either Dahlmann or Dolheimer, I don't remember the correct spelling. All I know was that he had a German last name and I was certain that he was from Minnesota or maybe from Milwaukee. One of his family's photos he had shown me was a big 18 wheelers truck with the Schlitz beer logo sign and his cousins and friends were surrounding the truck. I often wondered how he is doing and hoping that he is doing well....

Chapter Seven

In the spring of 1974, one of the
GI's introduced me to a young man who
had just got stationed to Korea. This GI,
Ricky, was a pretty good friend of mine
who checked in often to see how I was
doing. We were not sexually involved but
sometimes he helped me out with money
if I was really struggling. When I was
recovering from the carbon monoxide
poisoning, he brought me a puppy to
keep me company. The puppy was black
with large white spots and Ricky even
brought a large bag of puppy food with
him and we called him "pup". This little
pup inhabited part of the empty space
and the hollowness of my heart. Just
hearing 'pup's breathing helped me to
appreciate life again, and I appreciated
Ricky. With that said, the GI Ricky
introduces to me was from Kansas City,
Kansas and he had bright red hair, green
eyes, a face full of freckles, and his name
was Randy. I was grateful to meet
someone, and we started to date; four

months later we got engaged. Randy said
that he had a girlfriend name Sue in his
hometown but that he found out that she
moved on with Randy's best friend after
he got stationed in Korea. Maybe he
asked me to marry him out of
devastation from losing his girlfriend, or
even out of anger, or simply he was just
lonely. Understanding all of this, I said
"yes", by virtue saving myself from the
wretched life I was in. I am aware that
many people will chastise for what I did
and be that as it may be, I need to be
honest with whom reading my story.
Shortly after I got engaged to Randy, my
mother came to collect her monthly
allowance and brought me a letter from
Bong Song. I was dumbfounded to hear
from him after all these years and
wondered how this came about. I was
trembling with the fear as I opened the
letter.

The letter stated that he is ready to
accept me back as the care taker for his
aging mother and our two children, but in
the meanwhile he will continue to live

with his own family, which is his new wife and his other children. The letter also indicated that there is a "condition" to his acceptance. The condition of me fitting into his life, he indicated, was that it was essential that I'd kept myself pure since we got divorced, and that I needed to stay celibate as long as I am a caregiver for his family. I was dumbfounded by his request and my heart was racing like the fast train with the steam spewing out of the top of my head. How dare he? What made him think to send such a letter? I couldn't help but to think if my mother had something to do with it- did she beg him to take me back? Is it because she was afraid I may have the chance to leave Korea? With the hundreds of questions going through my mind, I still couldn't help thinking about my two boys. I had indubitable dreams to see my kids more than anything and I would gladly give up my life for them...except, I did not keep myself pure and I might be pregnant with Randy's child. Every defeat, every heart break and every loss...out of everything I had been through, there was no greater loss than losing any of my children forever and my heart was breaking into pieces all over again. My mother tried her best to convince me to return to Bong Song. I wrote a responding letter to him uttering "I sleep with hundreds of men". After that, I never heard from him again. I've carried guilt and sorrow for not being there for my two sons all throughout my life....and I will hold it to my dying day.

All these years, my father had no idea how I survived and I never saw him. When I reunited with my parents soon after Tom set me free from the hands of the Madam in the brothel, only my mother knew what happened to me from the time I had gone missing until the day I set out to leave the country. My second youngest sister lived with me and Randy until I left Korea, and I was hoping that someday I could send for her to come to the states. The marriage process with Randy took 8 months to complete and in June of 1975, I gave birth to our beautiful daughter. I named her Kelly and Randy gave her the middle name Sue. When she was just 6 months old Randy was ordered to return to the U.S., before the American Embassy had issued my visa, and Kelly and I were left behind.

Luckily, it only took two weeks to get my visa and then we were ready to depart from Korea. A week before I left the country, my mother finally told my father that I was married to an American soldier, that I had a baby girl and that I was leaving for America. Four days before our departure, my father came to see me and my daughter Kelly. I don't remember having much of a conversation with him, and he didn't show any emotion, no sadness or anger. He did hold Kelly once, and released a long sigh as he was holding her. The day of our departure, it was only my mother who came to say farewell at the Seoul airport. She was tearful and said "All I did was to take from you and now you are leaving for good and I am so sorry". I embraced her and sobbed with her. "I will see you again mom". As the plane peeled down the runway, I looked out the window as the tears rolled down to my cheeks. "Good bye my country" I thought, "I don't know if I'll ever come back but I am departing you to find my freedom and surpass my individuality." It was a long flight from Seoul, Korea to California and Kelly cried most of the flight. I was also having terrible air sickness and could not hold my head up. One of the stewardesses was kind enough to help take care of my daughter. When we got to San Francisco, I barley remember how I got my green card and got on the connecting flight to Kansas. On January 28, 1976, after 23 hours of long flights, me and my daughter finally landed in Kansas City, and I was 28 years old.

At the airport Randy and his parents were waiting for us. Randy's family seemed nice and they were happy to meet us. I believe Randy had 8 brothers and sisters, and all lived in Kansas except one of his younger sisters who lived in Harlingen, Texas. Randy's parents lived in a small house but were putting on an extension to have a larger kitchen and 2 more bedrooms; the bedrooms weren't finished and still had a dirt floor when we arrived. The rooms had no doors but we placed sheets for privacy and the three of us used one room with a bunk bed in it.. My mother-in-law was Irish and had bright red hair just like Randy and she weighed nearly 300 pounds. My father-in-law was thin and worked at some type of mill or factory and he said that he was part German. The family was very close to each other and fishing was their favorite sport. A month after we got to Kansas, Randy got stationed to Fort Hood, which was in Texas in a city called Killeen.

I was having difficulty adjusting to the new culture, extreme difficulty getting used to food other than Korean food. The sudden change of food made me ill, physically and emotionally, but there was no Korean store or restaurant nearby; I missed Korean food so desperately. It was a big hurdle to overcome the sudden change, it was almost like having a drug or alcohol withdrawal symptoms. After staying with Randy's parents for a month in Kansas, we set out on our journey to Fort

Hood driving an old blue Chevy Impala,
which Randy loved. Fort Hood was one
of the largest military bases in America.
It was something like a 16-18 hours'
drive from Kansas to Texas. On our way
there we stopped at a fast food
restaurant and Randy asked me if I was
hungry. In Korean culture if you are
asked if you were hungry, you would say
"I am okay" just to be polite. It is a stupid
culture if you think about it, but I didn't
know any better. In Korean culture even
if you said "I am okay" we figure he/she
probably hungry and we would go ahead
and offer something to eat or drink. To
my surprise, Randy got a big burger,
French fries and a big cup of soda for
himself and nothing for me. So, I starve
all day, but Kelly had milk to drink.

After the long drive we finally got
to Texas. Far from the military base, he
rented a rundown trailer in the middle of
nowhere for $85.00 month. The trailer
had no heat or hot water, and although
we were in Texas, the February-March
nights were cold. The floor of the trailer

was made creaking sounds with each footstep and some nights I could hear the howling wind against the thin siding. Randy took us to the Commissary for grocery shopping once a month when he got paid, and the rest of the time I had to manage the best way I could with a small child. Randy spent a lot of time outside of our home, going fishing or bowling with his buddies from the base. He would leave home at 4:30-5:00 in the morning and he did not return home often until close to midnight. I was often scared, being alone in the rundown trailer in the middle of nowhere, and we didn't have much to eat. I didn't know how to drive and regardless, we only had one car. Luckily, there was always a lot of fish in the fridge because Randy likes fishing. I had them for breakfast, lunch and dinner but I didn't mind too much. I did the laundry in the bathtub by hand and hung them outside to dry, which I didn't mind either because I was used to doing laundry by hand. However, being alone most hours of the day took a toll on my emotions. Then I realized that I was pregnant again. When I was about

six months into the pregnancy, Randy
announced that he was going to
Germany for six months to receive
special training. When he took me to the
military gynecologist for a follow up
appointment, I tried to explain to the
doctor that I was scared of being alone
with the small child and another baby on
the way. The doctor understood the
circumstances and wrote a letter to the
commanding officer.

The doctor said that it shouldn't be
any problem, and that Randy will be
excused from leaving the country under
the special circumstances. A month later
before the dawn, someone knocked on
our trailer door. When I opened the
door, a young lady stood on the wooden
stairs step and said, "Hi, I am Randy's
sister Brenda". Randy said that he made
arrangements with his sister Brenda for
me to stay with her and her boyfriend
for the next 6 months. He had not
mentioned anything about me and our
daughter going to live with Brenda for 6
months until after she arrived. That

morning, we packed our stuff and loaded into a small U-Haul truck, which she brought it with her. We attached Randy's blue Chevy Impala in back of the truck and headed out to Brenda's place in Harlingen, Texas, about 20 miles from the Mexican border. Randy seemed to be excited about his journey to Germany and hurried us on our way to his sister's home. Later I found the letter that the doctor wrote for Randy to be excused from going to Germany in his car unopened.

Four months after Randy left for Germany, I gave birth to a beautiful boy, and I named him Thomas. Two months after Tom was born, Randy returned to Texas and we were on our way back to Fort Hood. This time, we were able to move into military base housing and I was ever so excited. The house on the base had the two bedrooms, an open living and dining room, a small kitchen and even a laundry room I was overjoyed! Since we moved into the army base, I got to know more about the place which is/was the Army's premier installation facility to train and deploy heavy forces. The base is located on 214,968 acres and it is the only post in the United States capable of stationing and training two Armored Divisions. I also found out that the Killeen community is a model of support for Army families, including Korean businesses. Not long after we moved into base, I located Korean grocery stores, restaurants and even churches. I also found out that Fort Hood was named after Confederate General John Bell Hood who is best known for commanding the Texas brigade during the American Civil War.

The inside of the base housing was clean, bright and felt safe. There was a bus than ran through our street every hour of the day to town and to the inside the base Commissary (military grocery store). I was even more excited to find out there were other Korean women whom were married to American soldiers living on the base. Randy enjoyed his hobbies, fishing, hunting and bowling with his friends and I joined a Korean church, had friends to talk to and was able to eat Korean food, and Kelly had friends to play with in the neighborhood. Less than one year after we moved onto the base, I bumped into Randy's friend's wife who mentioned Randy departing for Germany less than three weeks from that day. I was shocked to hear this, because Randy did not mention anything about it. She realized it was news to me and said "oh, I am so sorry, I though you knew". She said that her husband is in Randy's division. I was upset with Randy for not telling me beforehand, but I could not stop him from leaving. He was never a good communicator to begin with but months went by and I did not hear from him. Kids birthdays and holidays came and went, but he never sent any cards for his children nor made a simple phone call to us. I was worried that something bad might have happened to him. I was finally able to get in contact with the commanding officer to let him know about my concern. Randy finally called me and stated that he was just "too busy" with work.

There were many Korean churches in Texas and I joined one of them close to our home. I learned how to drive with the help from one of girl from church and then I got my driver's license. At that it was a written test followed by a driving test. I scored 98 points on the written test, but the driving test I failed twice and then finally passed the third time. The testing police officer said that he was a little hard on me because he wanted to make sure that my kids were safe while I am driving and I appreciated his comments. When Randy returned home one year later, I found several photos of him with a woman who seemed to be his lover. One of his army buddies also told me that Randy is in love with the girl in Germany and he lived with her for the entire time he was there. I confronted Randy but he neither denied nor admitted this, but just walked away.

Not long after Randy came back from Germany, he got stationed to Fort Golden in Georgia, and we had to move again. There we rented a house but he did not stay with us as it was too far from the base, and he decided to stay in the army barracks. I converted the living room to an alteration/dress shop, got a sewing machine and put up a sign in front of the driveway, "K & T Alteration & Dress maker". I had a steady stream of customers and made some money to help out with the bills. I don't remember how long we were there, but soon Randy called to tell us we got housing on the base. Again, we packed our stuff and moved onto Fort Gordon in Augusta, GA. Then, one day Randy came home and stated that he was going back to Germany again, this time he was going for two years. I heard from his friends that the army will pay for the cost of moving, including airfare, for the entire family if Randy chose for us to do so. I told Randy that me and the kids would rather go to Germany with him than be left behind for 2 years, however, he tried to convince me that Germany was a "terrible place" for Korean women and he insisted on going there by himself. Now I knew he was going back there to be with his girlfriend and he may not come back to us. Since we could no longer live on the base if he was gone, we purchased a doublewide mobile home about a month before he left for Germany. We figured that I would be better off where they had a larger Korean community, so the home was on the outskirts of Savannah GA. I still remember the name of the trailer park "Ogeechee Road" with thick bamboo trees all around.

I remember the day we dropped off Randy at the airport. He said a quick goodbye to us before he hurried and disappeared into the crowd, like a little boy going to the amusement park. I felt empty and lost as I was driving back home with my two little kids. "Two years?" I thought, "how am I going manage for two years?" The paycheck from the army was divided into two, half went to Randy and half came for us. The half of the paycheck was not nearly enough for our mortgage and other living expenses. A few months had passed since Randy left and as usual, he stop contacting us and I didn't have any information on where he was. I was able to get a job at the Korean grocery store nearby, but after paying for a babysitter for two kids it wasn't even worth the trouble. I sometimes brought Tom with me to work to save money, but that the owner did not appreciate. The owner of the store, who was a Korean woman, also owned a restaurant and I worked there as a waitress in the evening. The money from both jobs helped pay the bills, but I was constantly worrying about leaving the kids with the sitter, who was teenager from our neighborhood.

The following summer, one afternoon, me and my kids were invited to a picnic with one of waitress at the restaurant. When we got there, she said they were actually going to picnic at the beach. I told her that we weren't prepared for going to the beach, but she insisted for us to come along and the kids were excited. She introduced me to her boyfriend's friend, whose name was Keith. Keith offered to purchase bathing suits with beach towels for us, which made my kids happy. After a fun day at the beach we all went to a local restaurant for dinner, and Keith generously paid the tab for us, and my kids seemed to like him. We started to talk about having a difficult time finding good babysitters, and Keith offered to watch my kids when he could.

Keith was a Marine, stationed on Paris Island doing office work and had been in the Marine Corp. for 13 years. He said that he served in Vietnam during the war, not in a combat zone but as the office clerk. Paris Island was in South Carolina, base where they had boot camp, and it was about an hour drive from us in Savanna. Six months had past and still no call from Randy, and I figured that he was with his girlfriend and living happily ever after. I am ashamed to admit that I somehow got involved with Keith. Nevertheless, he was a good caregiver for my two kids and I appreciated him for all he did for them and they liked him very much. That is no excuse for making the

mistake and I am truly guilty of what I
did.

To my surprise, Randy returned
home after spending less than a year in
Germany. I later learned from another
friend that his girlfriend broke up with
him and he returned home to see if he
could salvage what's left in our marriage.
Randy was depressed from losing his
girlfriend when he returned home. He
also found out that I was involved with
someone, which made him feel even
worse. I told him that I knew all about his
affair in Germany and I didn't think he
was ever coming back to us. Randy
suggested that we should take our kids to
Six Flags for a mini-vacation, and try to
work out our marriage for the children
sake. I told Keith that saving my family
was important to me and I needed to give
it a chance for my marriage with Randy.
Keith was distraught and left home
threatening to kill himself, but I knew by
his nature and personality he would
never harm himself. I believe it was
around August of 1981 at this time, and

Randy suggested we take out a loan for travel expenses and asked me to co-sign the loan for $2,000 with our furniture as collateral. In 1981 $2,000 was lot of money for us, but I want to do the right thing for our kids. A few days after getting the money, Randy spent some on Kelly for couple of outfits and a pair of shoes for starting first grade in September. Then he took the rest of the money and disappeared, without saying goodbye to me or the kids, and we never saw or heard from him again. He did not leave a penny for us. I was left alone with two children- Kelly was 5 and Tom was 3 ½ when Randy left us. The loan company began calling me day after day, demanding payment. They threatened me, indicating they would send a truck to pick up all of our furniture. I can't blame them for getting angry but I didn't know what I could do to solve the problem. I only had a 6th grade education and spoke limited English, with no specific job skills and no extended family to rely on.

Randy's family was never close to us, but after his disappearance, they completely cut off all communications. Needless to said that the only person I could turn in was Keith, whom I trusted with my kids. He was helpful with taking care of my kids when I had to work and they enjoyed being with him. I was grateful that he was around when we needed him. However, Keith had his own problems. I began to notice that regardless of the situation, his telling of lies about money became a routine and he actually believed his own lies. He ended up leaving the Marine Corp after 13 long years, and landed a job as a security guard. He then frequently bounced off from one job to another and lied about his paycheck being "screwed up" by payroll clerk. He began to steal things out of my home, such as taking a $50.00 bill from my wallet and then blamed it on his best friend. Another time he sold my lawnmower and then blamed it on a neighbor kid who was a young African American boy.

As much as I did not want to hurt my children's feeling, I tried to end the relationship with Keith, but he was unwilling to give up. At that time, we were attending a Salvation Army church because they had an after-school program free of charge and they were diligent about children's welfare. Their logo was "heart to God and hand to men" and I was grateful for their work. I volunteered my time on Sundays to work with children as a "sunbeam school" teacher which is the same as the "Sunday school" in Christian churches. Once, I wore a Salvation Army uniform and went to a rally in Chalet, North Carolina to represent our sunbeam school. During that time Keith must have discussed our situation to the church minister, who we called Lieutenant S. The minister then began to visit my home, and started counseling me about "faith" in God. He said that Keith was remorseful for what he did and insisted that I should forgive him if I truly believe in God. He also convinced me that I needed to make the relationship legal by marrying Keith because it is the right thing to do in God's eyes. After all these years, my mind is still culturally bound by old belief and now I am a Christian, and I felt I had to do the right thing to please God. So, we had a small wedding ceremony at the church attend by the minister, his wife, my two kids and a couple of my friends. Lieutenant S. and his wife were honest, good people and I am sure they did what they believed was the right thing to do. However, I believe everything happened for the reason and I hated myself for doing so.

When Kelly was 10 and Tom was 8, I had another child which is my youngest son, and named him Kirk. We were living in Hilton Head Island, SC at the time because I was working there as a hostess for one of the busiest Japanese restaurants in town. The Japanese steak house, called Makoto, was owned by a Caucasian man named Mr. Smith and his family. There was only one Japanese chef who was the head cook, and all the other chefs were Korean or other ethnicities Most of the waitresses were Korean

women. Mr. Smith was a man with a
sense of humor, and he was generous to
his employees. We reported to work
early, so the chef could prepare dinner
for all of us before the restaurant opened
for business. He did the same after each
shift was over in the evening, and we all
enjoyed food and each other's company.
It was a great working environment and I
didn't mind working hard. Mr. Smith
hired me as a hostess, wearing a long
kimono with pinned up hair and high
sandals. Mr. Smith let me adjust my job
title as the time went by to fit my
situation, especially after I was pregnant
with my third child. When I was 7 months
pregnant, he let me work as a cashier as it
was easier on my feet. I also cleaned his
restaurant 7 days a week to earn extra
income and he paid me well Hilton Head
Island was a tourist place with golf
courses, tennis courses and was often
visited by celebrities for tournaments.
One time I met Ron Howard from "Happy
Days", who was visiting the island with
his wife for a celebrity golf tournament.
Keith worked as security guard at a gated
community call Wax-Ford Plantation,

where millionaires lived with man-made
lagoon and yachts. He was able to keep
his job for entire year with good health
insurance. Keith keeping his job allowed
me to have the baby comfortably, without
worrying about the hospital bill.

I must say that Keith was not a "bad
person" but he had serious mental health
issues, which even a therapist could not
help. One time he told us that he bought a
small house with a V.A. loan, and showed
me the paper work, which I didn't
completely understand. One day he took
me and our children to show us the
outside of the house that he presumably
bought. He said that the closing was
another month away and people are still
living in the house. I asked him to make
an appointment to see the inside of the
house, but each time we scheduled to see
the place, something always "came up"
and we were unable to view. However, I
still believed in him and I was just happy
to have place of our own, and I didn't care
what the inside looked like. I am a good
interior designer and know I can always

make place nice. We all waited impatiently, including Keith and the moving day finally arrived. As I am writing this, I feel so stupid, but I didn't think anyone would lie about something like that. Early in the morning, Keith left to pick up the key for our new home and the moving truck. We were all packed and waiting, but the time past to noon, and then past 4:00 pm, but no Keith. Then I realized "oh my lord, he lied again"...but who would make up a lie about something like that I thought. I never asked him to buy us a house, or complained about where we lived, so why on earth?? He walked through the door when the dusk started to set in. He hung his head low and with a small, still voice "I am sorry...". The rest is history, because I can't even begin to tell you what we had to go through, not to mention how his actions hurt my innocent kids!

After the house incident, Keith seemed to be trying hard to make it things right. One day he said that we should move to Massachusetts where he was born and raised. His parents and other extended family all lives in MA, and he told me his parents would help us to start fresh. He also said that he already talked to his father and he agreed to help us by sending him his credit card, which had a $5,000 limit. He said that we will have to make the payments, but it could help pay for moving expenses. He had already gotten an estimate for the cost of a rental truck, and said we would be all set to go as soon as credit card arrived. 3-4 days later, Keith started to check the mailbox every for week. He then called his father in front of me and had a conversation about the mail being delayed. He told his father that he will definitely pay him back as soon as we settled down and we would take over the payments. He sounded so sincere and said "thank you dad, I love you" and hung up the phone. Two weeks went by after having the conversation with his dad still no mail and no credit card... you guessed it, he lied again. It turned out that Keith talking on the phone with his dad was all an act without having anyone on the other line. Don't get me wrong, Keith was not a malicious person. I did not understand then, but now I know he had a serious mental illness, but it does not make it right for our family to suffer, especially our children.

Another time, I was setting in the car at a parking lot at the store to feed our baby (Kirk). Suddenly, a police officer knocked on the window. As I rolled down the window and in a puzzled tone said "Yes, officer?" he asked "Are you Un Chu Eldridge?" When I said "yes" he responded, "Please get out of the car, you are under arrest". I was shocked and asked him what I did to be arrested. He said I was under arrest "for writing a bad check". Later I realized that the checks from work that Keith should have deposited to our bank account, he somehow cashed and spent. Serendipitously, when the officer took me into the station and asked the clerk at the front desk to "book her" and call child services for the baby, the clerk asked him "did you read her rights?" When he responded "oh no, I didn't" the clerk said "well than I can't book her and you need let her go".

Even with all of these things happening, I began to study to earn my citizenship. The day of the test, we drove to Charleston S.C. and I was in front of a Judge, who was the tester. I was so nervous; I felt like I was going to pee my pants, but I cracked big smile at the judge. It must be the nervous reaction, but the judge looked at me and said "lady, you have a million-dollar smile". Once I was at ease the judge asked me only three questions. "What are the branches of the U.S. government, and what are their responsibilities? Another question was "What is the name of our first lady?" which was the 40th first lady Nancy Reagan. Then he asked me to write "I love America" and I passed it!! He said "Congratulations" and shook my hand. It was February 28, 1986 when I was sworn in as a proud citizen of America; where the milk and honey floated, the "promised land".

Chapter Eight

After years of dealing with Keith's
behavior and its repercussions, which
included me getting arrested for writing
bad checks, moving 13 times, large debts
and more, my depression, anxiety and
panic symptoms had gotten worse, but I
didn't understand the concept or how to
deal with my emotions. I felt bad for
Keith being who he was and it tore me
apart for causing emotional pain to our
children, and I couldn't handle it any
more. Keith decided to return to
Massachusetts to live with his parents
and said "I will straighten things out for
us". After he left, I was able to get into
low income housing and continue to
work at the restaurant as a waitress as
well as keep the cleaning job 7 days week,
and we survived. Although Keith was in
Mass, we kept in contact. One day he
called me and said that he sent greeting
cards for the kids because he missed

them, and each had $5.00 bills in the card. I was appreciative for his thoughtfulness, and looked for the cards to arrive. I looked for the damn cards three weeks and darned on me that he lied again. He blamed it on the postal worker who must have stolen the cards and kept the money. I wanted to scream, curse every bad word there was to curse because I felt like my brain was about to explode into pieces. I didn't understand Why? Why would you lie about something like that for what reason? Why did I keep on believing him? "Am I stupid? An idiot?" I thought... "what the f...k was wrong with me?!!"

I was ashamed myself for keep disappointing my kids for no good reason. Kelly was about 13, Tom was 11 and Kirk had just turned 2 years old when Kirk came down with the strange illness. I took him to the doctor and the doctor said he just had the flu, but the inside of Kirk's mouth was full of sores and he could not eat and was having trouble drinking any liquid for weeks. He was getting weak, could not stand up, lost a lot of weight and kept asking for his dad. I was afraid that God was punishing me through my child for splitting up with Ken and called him to let him know that Kirk was sick. He suggested I bring the kids to Massachusetts, at least for little while until Kirk got better. He said that Massachusetts had the best doctors and he also wanted to see his son. So, I took a leave of absence from work and with the three kids we were on the plane to Massachusetts, where we never been before.

When we got to Massachusetts, we stayed with Keith's parents and met his extended family. Keith's parents were in their 60's and lived in Lynn, MA in the same house Keith grew up, finished high school and joined the Marine Corps. His father was a kind and hard-working man who proudly showed me his photos from when he was in the Navy. He was now retired from the mill working industry and continued to work part time as a bartender at the local oldies bar. He was an honest and kind gentleman, whereas Keith's mother was unkind and moody, and didn't like my children including her own grandson Kirk. It seemed the only people she liked was her daughter and their family who were financially successful. She even had two different cookie jars, one for her daughter's kids with name brands and another for my kids which the cheapest brands in the store; this even my kids still remember. Keith's family all admitted that he had some problems but insisted that "all he needed was have a good woman to change him". His father wanted us to move to Mass permanently, where he said they had the best schools for kids and better job opportunities for me, and it sounded attempting.

Since Keith and I were separated and not divorced, we left Kelly and Tom with his parents, went back to S.C., rented a big truck and moved to Mass, and by that time Kirk got well. Keith was working at a Richdale store as manager and I got a job as a cashier at the same

store. About six months later I was
promoted to the manager's position and
Keith got transferred to a bigger store as
manager and with both of our incomes
we were able to move out of his parent's
home. However, when I took over the
store as manager, I did an audit and
noticed over $500.00 was missing from
the store account and reported this to the
main office. I was ashamed to find out
that Keith was responsible for the
missing cash. Keith had a sob story about
why he had to take the money and
promised to pay it back in full. The top
management was kind enough to put
Keith on probation and let him meet the
job.

Eventually, Keith lost his job, so we
moved again to the next town and he
worked as a security guard and I got a job
as a nursing assistant at a nursing home.
About five months later I was promoted
to activity assistant, which I enjoyed very
much. While I was working at the nursing
home, there was a moment that I felt
degraded by an old male patient. I was

fully uniformed as a CNA with the name badge and was walking down the hallway when I spotted the male patient, probably in his 80's. He was in the bathroom with the door open and as I passed by, he waved $5.00 bills and motioned with his index finger for "come over here". I was so shocked and humiliated; I just ignored him and walked away. I couldn't help but wonder and think "he must have been to Korea when he was a young soldier" and maybe he was remembering the days of "camp towns". I was not behaving in any way to cause the scene but those things happened to me more than once. Was I cursed by some kind fealty spirit? Despite that incident most of my working experience at the nursing home was a pleasant one. There was a female patient who became blind at her old age. She was a retired school teacher and I often visited her before the end of my shift. She was wise and I loved to chat with her and hear her experiences as a school teacher. She was never married and she had no family so she appreciated my attention. She could not see how I looked but she recognized me by my walking steps and sound. When I got closer to her room, she softly called out "is it you One Two?" She could not pronounce my name Un Chu and that is the name she used, One Two.

However, Keith could not keep up with any job for a long period of time and we moved a few more times before we ended up in a low-income housing complex in Peabody, MA. The housing was a brand-new complex with three bedrooms, a laundry facility and a small back yard and we were thrilled. Unfortunately, Keith continued his behaviors. Just about every other week he said something "happen" to his paycheck, either someone stole his money or the payroll department "messed up" his hours and he didn't get paid. He lied about things that he had no reason to lie about, but he did anyways and sometimes he believed his own lies. He lied to our children, minister at our church, neighbors and friends and I begin to experience headaches and often memory loss. I would be driving and suddenly I can't remember where I was

199

going and it scared me. Keith was not a
church goer and usually me and the kids
will attend. However, that particular day,
he took our two boys to church after
having an argument with me. Kelly was
out with her friends and I was home
alone. I was writing a poem and I felt sad,
hopeless and just want to go to sleep for a
"long time". I seriously wasn't trying to
kill myself, but just want to forget
everything for "just for a while". I look
through the medicine cabinet in the
bathroom and found the bottle of cough
medicine plus two boxes of
antihistamines and took them all. It must
an early into the evening and Kelly came
home from her friend's house and found
me unconscious. She said she was
hysterical and called 911. When the
police and EMT showed up and found the
poem I have written, they stated "it was
suicidal attempt". When I woke up from
the hospital, I was at the psychiatric unit
on "suicide watch". I was told that they
had pump my stomach, made me drink
some awful tasting drinks and could not
leave the hospital for 3 days. Needless to
said, my children were more than just

upset with me. They felt "abandonment" by their own mother who try to escape all by herself from harshen life by ending her life. I felt so guilty for what I have done and I couldn't blame them for feeling deserted. They must have been so scared and terrified, especially my daughter who found me passed out in the darkened room.

In 1990 just before Kirk started Kindergarten, Keith and I were divorced. We have shared custody with Kirk and he was ordered to pay child support but he eventually left the state to avoid paying and started a new life elsewhere. While this was going on my depression had gotten worsen and income I was making was not enough to take care of our household of 4 people. Although, we lived in at the low-income housing, I always worked and never sought for any other assistance, but it came to the point that I finally convinced myself that we needed some extra help.

It was a winter morning as I got on the bus and headed out Salem MA where the welfare office was located. When I got there, people were already lined up, mostly young women with kids. I waited hours until finally my name was called, and I sat in front of a middle-aged woman with tight curly red hair. She gave me the looks of "what the hell you want?" It felt like it was taking forever for her to review my paper work and she kept asking questions in a sarcastic way. It seemed like a grueling interview and I burst out crying because I was so ashamed. She finally handed me a $53.00 voucher and I walked out feeling degraded. When I walked out of the welfare office it was snowing like crazy. Now I had to go the local bank and exchange voucher for food stamps. In those days they did not have EBT cards that you could just swipe at the grocery store and be done with. Also, not every bank had a food stamps exchange system, only a few selected banks. At the bank, there were two lines, one for regular business and another for food stamps.

As I was standing in line, I felt like everyone's eyes were piercing at me. I exchanged my voucher to food stamps, one $20.00 voucher, two $10.00 vouchers and two $5.00 vouchers, all in a paper food stamps booklet. I had never used them before and I was nervous and also afraid that someone I know would see me using the food stamps. So, I got on the bus and went to the next town Lynn. I remembered when we were living in Lynn, I used to see many shoppers using the food stamps. While I was waiting in the cashier's line at the store, I looked into my cart and thought "Am I getting the right items?" There was a bottle of soda, hostess cupcakes and some chips for my kids; I wondered what people would think I was misusing the government money. After all items were rung up, I handed the food stamps booklet to the cashier. She looked at me as she was annoyed and "you need to tear them yourself!" and hastily I tore them to give to her. Now she was even more frustrated, and got on the microphone in a loud voice "Food stamp change at the isle 7!" I felt like I wanted to crawl under somewhere to hide and never again did I seek any assistance other than our low-income apartment.

I worked as a housekeeper, seamstress, personal care attendant and even as a security guard once. I made sure that my children were fed, clothed and once I learned that they have to stand on separate line for kids who are using vouchers, I made sure they were provided lunch money. My children were grateful for what they had and their friends felt comfortable staying over at our home. They were always enjoyed my cooking.

Oh, I have funny story to tell - when I was doing security at an inpatient psychiatric hospital, I was at the detox department watching over a man who was just brought into the unit for an evaluation. He looked over six feet tall, and had red hair with a scruffy beard, and was restless, trying to leave the area. I asked him nicely "Can you please sit down?" he then looked at me with sneer and replied "What are you going to do about it? ha!" Then he said "I suppose you know Karate?" I quickly stood up straight, put my hands on my hips and raised tone of my voice "Do you want to find out?!" He suddenly plopped down on the chair and waived his hands and said "Oh no, that's okay I will sit down".

The project home in Peabody was a safe haven for me and my children for nearly 10 years. Our monthly rent was 33% of my income plus utilities and we were able to stay there longer than any other of our previous homes and we were grateful. There were 23 units in the projects, filled with one Vietnamese family who had five girls, two African American families, us (which Asian mother with three mixed race children) and all the rest were Caucasian families. Most people in the neighborhood were friendly, especially our next-door neighbor with three kids. The man of that household worked for the city and his wife worked at the country club. They were always nice to our kids and the husband had a great sense of humor. We all had a fenced backyard, and I planted flowers, shrubs and a finger size pine tree Kirk got from McDonald, which grew about 3 feet tall by the time we left the neighborhood. Tom said he passed by the neighborhood not too long ago and saw our little tree had grown to over 10 feet tall. From that project home Tom got accepted to UMass Amherst to study pre-med, Kelly got married to her high school sweetheart and Kirk grew up and started the high school. I worked full time at a dry cleaner, which was owned by a Korean couple, and I also worked part time at the convenient store on weekends and some evenings, and I was able to purchase a used car. I appreciated very much our comfortable living space, but on the other hand I wanted so much more, for us to be able to get out of the projects.

I knew my kids were bullied in school, especially in high school. Peabody High School was located in West

Peabody, which is an area known for "rich neighbors" and the students from that area were not so kind to kids from South Peabody, especially kids from project homes. I remember when Kelly was in high school, she missed all of her classes for an entire week, and I didn't know about it until the truant officer from school knocked on our door. I was startled to hear that she was skipping school because she left every morning as usual. I was sure there was a good reason for what she did but I was outraged. I also found out that she was staying at her best friend's home instead of going to school. As most of mothers do, instead of taking responsibility I blamed her best friend. I told Kelly that her friend was a "bad influence" and she is not allowed to see her anymore. Kelly tried to explain that she was being bullied at school and her friend Tara was just helping her out, but I didn't want to hear it. I gave an ultimatum to Kelly, it was either me and stay home or her friend Tara, and guess what? she chose her friend Tara and left home. I was upset and sad at the same time, but I knew where she was staying and I left it be. About a week later, I found her sleeping on the couch when I came home from work. I was so happy and went out and got her a bouquet of flowers, gave her a hug and we both cried. Kelly's best friend Tara is still her best friend after 26 years and I am so glad that Kelly chose her over me. She was the maid of honor at Kelly's wedding and they stood by each other for "better or for worse" and I love them dearly. One thing I regret is that Kelly's friend T. went through a lot since her teenage years in her personal life, losing both parents and all, but I was not there for her as I should have. I was just too busy taking care of my own kids. Nevertheless, she has a wonderful and sweet family of her own and they are very happy, which eases my mind. Kelly have many good friends throughout her life from High School to adulthood friends, Amanda, Cindy and many others and happy to know that they are all doing well and I love and appreciate them all.

Eventually the time came and I had
no choice but to move out of our little
"safe haven", because I now only had one
child Kirk at home and we were no
longer legible for three-bedroom
housing. Nonetheless, I was dating a
successful and moderately good-looking
Jewish man name Jacob who was 8 years
older than I was. I met him when I was
working second shift at the convenience
store as a second job. Jacob who was
5'11", and he thought I was about 5'8"
tall because I was standing on a platform
behind the counter where I worked. On
our first date he was shocked to found
out that I was only 5 ft. tall. Even though I
wore high heel shoes, the first words that
came out of his mouth were "What the
hell happened to your legs?" but me
being short didn't stop us for having a
pleasant evening and we continued to see
each other. Jacob had white hair, he was
older looking then his actual age and I
looked 10 years younger than my age.
Therefore, from others point of view we
appeared 20+ years in age difference and
some viewed me as I was a "gold digger".
Was I? Jacob had never been married and

had no children. He said that he never
dated woman with children because he
did not care for kids. There had been
some ups and downs but our relationship
lasted and he introduced me to his
parents (father & step mother), other
extended family members, and his close
friends. His paternal aunt, who was in her
80's, loved me at the first sight, and
hoped that her nephew would finally
settle down. Jacob said that his aunt
practically raised him after his mother
was institutionalized when he was just a
toddler. He said that his mother suffered
from postpartum depression and she
often left him unattended. There was a
time that his father was away for a
business trip and Jacob was left alone in
the house for days, until his aunt found
him. Jacob was about 3 years old when
that happened.

He said that her symptoms had gotten
worse as time passed, and that eventually
she had to have a lobotomy. I met her
before she passed away at the nursing
home where she had been bed-ridden for

over 30 years. He said that his mother does not remember him, but he continued to visit on her birthdays and Mother's-day since he was 18 years old. He said that before he turned 18, his father hadn't allowed him to see her. I felt so sad for him when I heard his story, and the empathy turned into love...and when she passed away, I was at his side at her burial but no one else came to pay the respect, just me and Jacob.

When Kelly got married and Tom went to college, Jacob decided that it was time to move forward with our relationship. He bought me a diamond ring and said that Kirk and I could move in with him. I gladly gave away all my furniture, dishes and stuff to my neighbors. I took bags of clothing and our memorable items, and left the street feeling like Cinderella. Pulling into the driveway of our new home, I felt that all my troubles were now behind us. I truly appreciated and loved Jacob for providing a good home, and then he took us on a trip to Florida to see his parents, in their mansion like home. Jacob was a regional manager at a stock brokerage company; he always dressed nice and drove a nice car with a car phone, which not too many people had at that time. His aunt and the rest of the family were kind and caring and welcomed me and my children with open arms. We celebrated the Passover at his aunt's house, attended family Bar Mitzvahs, attended family weddings and I quickly adopted his Jewish traditions.

I loved Jewish traditions because they had many similarities to Korean traditions. Jacob's aunt was an obstinate, strong willed (in a good way) woman just like my grandmother and she was highly respected by all her family members. She shared her recipes for matzo ball soup, borscht soup, fruit squares... Jacob was the only biological child to his father. His father, Aaron, was a retired lawyer from well-known law practice in the downtown of Peabody. He won a largely recognized case at the time, which was 'City vs. Eastman Gelatin" and he profited millions. He had now retired to Florida with his second wife, whom had three children from her previous marriage. Aaron was thrilled to find out that his stubborn son finally found someone to settle down with. He was delighted when we brought Kirk with us to visit their home in Florida. Jacob and his step mother never got along well, and they had a long history of him being oppositional towards her and she hated him.

The six months has passed since we moved into Jacob's house and I began to notice Kirk's behavior were changing drastically. He seemed to be depressed, was having trouble sleeping and his school grades were failing, but he refused to talk about what was going on. His school guidance counselor contacted me and suggested that Kirk should be seen by an individual therapist. Since it was suggested by the school counselor, I found a therapist for him, about an hour drive from where we lived. I was afraid that someone may find out that he was in counseling, and he may get teased or be ashamed. Several weeks into counseling, Kirk was referred to a female psychologist in Salem MA. The psychologist explained that Kirk was being verbally and psychologically abused by Jacob, along with physical aggression. The psychologist informed me that she was getting ready to file a 51A on us. That means DCF (The Department of Children and Family Services) would be involved, and Kirk could be taken away from me and placed in a Foster home.

It was known that Jacob disliked children, and he at times was verbally abusive to both of us. He would also grab Kirk's arms and display other physical aggressions without actually hitting him or me. He once threw a telephone because one of his stocks was down and hit the side of my face. However, it was unintentional and I didn't say anything. Jacob had lot of good traits but he was also controlling. He complained about the way I dressed, did my hair and

sometimes the type of shoes I wore. He
once bought me a pair of white platform
crocs that looked like nurse's shoes. He
asked me to wear them with the white
tube socks and short pants and he loved
it. He also got me a notebook to record
the mileage that I used with my own car. I
had to write dates, hours and the mileage
from home to my destinations, so he
could keep an eye on my usage of the car.
My car was not leased or rented but he
wanted to make sure that I was not
wasting mileage for no good reason.

When I confronted Jacob about the
way he treated Kirk, he did not deny his
actions, but stated that Kirk would never
amount to anything and that he needed
discipline. He demanded that I should
send him to a residential school facility,
similar to a military school to "toughen
him up". I knew Kirk was not athletic or
in the popular group like Jacob wished,
but I also knew that he had severe
Anxiety with panic symptoms, and he
would never survive in such a restricted
environment. I remember when he was in

Jr. High school, I pushed him to join the football team. Every weekend before the practice, he would have headaches, stomach aches with nausea, diarrhea and vomiting, and he end up quitting the team. I know what anxiety can do to people because I suffered the same symptoms for most of my life, but I never told anyone. Whenever I faced the difficult situation, my mouth dried up, heart beat raced and I would feel like it was going to jump out of my chest and that I could actually hear the thumping sound inside my ear drums. Sometimes I would have tunnel vision and even black out for a few seconds when I got too anxious. So, sending my child away to an unknown environment before an adult age was unthinkable for me. I contested to Jacob that I would never send Kirk to any such program and he gave me an ultimatum; to choose either him or my child. Here is the answer for those who considered me as gold-digger- earlier. No amount of luxury is worth sacrificing any of my children's wellbeing.

That evening, I packed several trash bags of clothes, gave back the engagement ring and we left Jacob's house onto the street. For the next 4 months, Kirk lived with his friend's family in a trailer park on the east side of the school and I went back and forth to my son Tom's apartment in Revere. Tom changed his major to computer science, got a well-paying job and got his first own apartment; I was so proud of him. Tom is a loving, caring and hard-working son who always worried about my wellbeing, even as small child. Once when he was about 3 years old, I had stomach pain and he ask me what was wrong with me. I told him "mommy's belly hurts". Then he walked away and returned a few minutes later. He said "open your hand mommy" and he put 2 tablets of aspirin in my hands, saying "Take this and go to sleep" as he gently stroked my hair. I am not sure how he got into the medicine cabinet, but I never forgot how sweet he was.

Several years later I heard news that Jacob's aunt passed away, and also that two of her daughters passed away, one from cancer and another from an auto accident. I felt sad for them because they were decent people. I also heard from one of Jacob's good friends that Jacob married his best friend's widow 'Ching', who was Chinese and disliked me and my children while her husband was alive and I was dating Jacob. Ching and her husband lived in a big beautiful house; he was a real estate developer and she worked at the Chinese restaurant as a hostess. Then somehow her husband lost his fortune and died from a brain tumor/cancer. Before he was diagnosed with the cancer, we all went out to the restaurant for dinner. After ordering dinner, I heard Ching and Jacob started to criticize my daughter Kelly, like I was invisible. I got really upset and walked out of the restaurant before dinner was served. I did not have my car at the time nor I had cell phone and I didn't have money to call for taxi, so I sat out on the sidewalk until they were done with dinner. Jacob never came out to check on me. However, I heard that after Jacob married Ching, he had lingering health issues and lost all of his millions in the stock market for making poor choices in investments. Trust me, I do not wish anyone misfortune, rather I pray for their health and prosperity, because in the same sense, I don't want anyone to wish me or my children's misfortune.

With that said, after leaving Jacob, I landed my very first mental health job at an agency called Health & Education Services, working for one of their group homes in Nike Village. Nike Village is a site in Topsfield MA, and it was named for the former Nike Nuclear Missile launcher site at the end of the road, which was built in the mid-1950's. The housing units were originally built for officers based at the site, which was active until 1974 and the launch site had its control center nearby in Danvers (B-05). The property was then used by the Army reserves from 1976-1990, and since then it has been leased by various social service agencies, and we were one of them. Health and Education Services, Inc. operated a number of community residences and supportive housing programs for clients of the Department of Mental Health. Nike Village, a converted military housing complex consisted of densely congregated "single family" ranch style homes, and hosted two transitional housing programs. The programs are designed to provide a bridge between institutionalized living (such as in hospitals or prisons), and community residences. The Tim-shell program provides services for individuals with severe mental health needs complicated by substance abuse issues. The Plowshares program, in which I got hired to work, was designed for individuals with less severe, but still significant mental illness and serious substance abuse issues. The director of the program Judy was a kind woman with the gentle spirit who gave me an opportunity while I was working toward getting GED. Even though, I didn't have prior work

experience as a mental health worker,
she hired me and became my mentor to
excel in the field. Another program was
located at the bottom of the street called
Serenity Supportive Housing, and this
program was for HIV/AIDS infected
individuals with mental health issues.

While I was working at the
Plowshares program, I volunteered to
cook Korean meals for the entire
residence at the Serenity Support house.
They all enjoyed this, and made me a
certificate of "appreciation". The
Plowshares program where I worked
consisted of 14 male and female clients
from ages 18 to 50+. Part of my job was
driving a 15 passengers van with
transporting clients to appointments, AA
meetings and to day programs and back. I
also did the weekly grocery shopping and
prepared meals for clients and staff. Soon,
I was put in charge of the food budget,
and was trained and received an ID for
access to the Food Bank in Boston. I was
able to save up money from the monthly

budget, and use it to celebrate the holidays and have summer cookouts for the residents.

I had a lovely co-worker name Mary and we often worked together on weekend and evening shifts. I remember the time we ran around and gathered flowers...yellow and purple mixed with the green leaves. We decorated the empty water bottles as the base and made flower arrangements for each female resident for their room. On these excursions we sometimes spotted the overgrown roughage, a tangled mess that covered an old abandoned bunker, reminding us of the missile base that once existed. Sometimes I took overnight shifts so I would have a place to stay at night instead of driving all the way to Revere.

Not long after I started working at Nike Village, I learned about a woman name Marie Balter. She happened to live in Topsfield, not too far from our facility. I heard that she was an orphan who was adopted by an unmarried alcoholic mother, who then turned her over to a foster home. Marie spent the first 20

years of her adult life in a mental
institution with the misdiagnosis of
schizophrenia. Despite that, she was able
to overcome her strife and study
psychology and eventually graduate
school at Harvard University. She later
became a well-known crusader for the
mentally challenged population for the
remainder of her life. She died while I
was working at the Nike Village and the
leftover food from the ceremony service
was donated to our program. I read her
obituary and watched the movie called
"Nobody's Child" cast by Marlo Thomas in
1986. The movie was nominated for 2
Golden Globes awards, another 4 wins
and 1 nomination. As our clients and staff
all gathered around sharing the leftover
meal, her courageous story deeply
touched my heart. Although, I did not
know her personally, her story not only
touched my heart but left a lasting
impression. It became a compass for
navigating my purpose in life and the
path to my redemption.

After 4 months of struggling without having my own place, I finally got into an income-based apartment in Peabody called Crown In Shield. It was an old mill building that was converted to a loft apartment and Kirk and I moved in. From there, I completed the GED course within 7 months while I was continues working at the Nike Village. I was chosen among 60 graduates to speak at the graduation ceremony in front of some 200 guests, including teachers, the superintendent and the city mayor. I was so nervous and I practiced my speech in front of our clients at the Nike Village. One client asked me "Are you leaving us?" and a few girls shed tears. All my children and my 2-year-old granddaughter from Kelly sat in the front row of guests, seats and listened to my first public speech. Kelly sobbed as I went on with my heart felt speech that jerked tears from many other people, including my teachers and superintendent....."I am ever so grateful for the opportunity....not to be enchained by the illiteracy...and God Bless America..."

It seemed like an endless amount of time has passed by... me and my children were always poor but the four of us built a life with love and perseverance and I am so proud of my children and our ever-growing family. My children suffered so much because of my incompetency in making many wrong life choices, but they never once complained or blamed me for it. We moved 18 times, and Kelly and Tom had to change school 13 times before they finished high school, but all my children have grown up to be loving, kind and hard-working individuals. I remember the time that Kelly was getting married. I made her wedding dress, intending to save money, but I actually ended up spending more. The wedding dress fitted top was carefully inlaid with pearls, like white beads that covered the entire top bodice, sewed by my hands. Her feminine waistline ascended to a bell shaped while a long and full skirt spilled down to her feet and the long train that channeled a Cinderella-like silhouette and she was beautiful in it. The hemline was adorned with laces and sequins that matched her veil, which I also designed and handmade. The half part of her hair was placed in an up-do with curls draped down to the side of her pretty face and she reminded me of the princess bride. Tom looked so handsome, wearing a black tuxedo as he embraced his sister's arm, walking her down the aisle to give her away to her husband. Kirk was the ring bearer, proudly wearing the same designed tuxedo, just like his brother.

The parents of the groom generously offered to pay the cost of wedding because our side had fewer guests, aside from not having money. I paid for the flower arrangements, photos and the tuxedos for my two sons and I wore a green velvet dress that I had previously purchased from the thrift store to attend a Christmas party for my work. I felt stupid for wearing a velvet dress because it was the end of August and it was too heavy for the weather. What can I say? I often do stupid things and later regretted my choice, but I am only a human. Regardless, it was a beautiful wedding ceremony. A couple of Kelly's bridesmaids and the Maid of Honor are still Kelly's best friends, after 24 years. Kelly's in-laws treat my daughter like their own child, they are a close family and we see each other on every family occasion and more. Kelly has 2 children, and my granddaughter is engaged to be married and they have a beautiful daughter. This makes my daughter a "grandma" and me a "great grandma". My granddaughter is beautiful, smart and a hard worker and she is an awesome mom, just like her mom. Her baby has blue eyes, she is so beautiful and precious. My granddaughter studied Early Childhood development and works for a nursery school as a second stage teacher. My grandson is in college, majoring in computer science like his uncle Tom and always work hard when he is home on vacation. Kelly and her husband are still in love with each other after 24 years of marriage, and they are an awesome parent to their two wonderful children. Kelly also went back to school and earned a degree to be a medical assistant and works for a General Surgery office in NH and she loves her job. My son-in law is a project manager for a local industrial sprinkler system company and he stays very busy. They recently sold the house they raised their two children in and purchased a bigger property further into NH to have their own little farm.

Tom later changed his major from pre-med to computer science and worked at a co-op for school internet services while he was studying at UMass. I enjoyed making his favorite meals and sending them along with him with the clean laundry when he visited home on weekends for his first year in college. While Tom was in the co-op at UMass Amherst, I decided to search for Randy, to give a chance for Kelly and Tom to know who their father is. Since Tom was working with the internet system at school, he was able to locate his aunt who lived in Harlingen, TX, and gave the information to me.

After many attempts I finally contacted her but she was reluctant to give out information about her brother. I told her that I was not looking for any retribution from her brother but simply wanted my children to know who their father was. I also told her that Kelly is married and Tom is in college and we are doing okay. She still refused to provide her brother's information, but later I received a call from Randy's father. He informed me that his wife which was my ex mother in law have passed away. He also informed me that Randy has remarried, had three sons and lived in Arkansas. After much conversation Randy's father, gave me the number to contact Randy, which I did. I spoke with Randy briefly after all those years of absence. Randy offered no apology for leaving us stranded with unpaid bills or taking the loan money, and he carried on conversation like nothing ever happened. He mostly talked about his three sons, his wife and their life in Arkansas. I gave him the contact number for Kelly and Tom and I left it up to him. A week later Tom called me from his school and said that Randy called him "collect" at his dorm, because Randy does not want to pay for the long-distance call. Shame on him!! I could not believe what I was hearing but it was the truth.

Tom was known to work and study hard, and even before his graduation, he had 4 job interviews lined up. I remember when he was going for first job interview; I got his only suit all pressed up from the dry cleaner where I had worked for 4 years. I was so proud of him as I sent him off to the interview. Even before he had a chance to go for a second interview, he got an offer from his first interview as an entry level offer for $50,000 a year. It was 18 years ago and to us, it was lot of money. I was ecstatic, because it was more money than we had ever dreamed of. "Take the job, take it" I excitedly told him, and without going for second interview Tom accepted the first job. 18

years later, he still works for the same company and of course, he has been promoted several times to higher levels. He is now one of the senior managers, overseeing staff across company locations, even in India.

As I began to share before, Tom was always protective of me as he was growing up. When he was 3 years old his father was playing with him and accidentally dropped him on the floor which broke his leg. We took him to the army doctor who said that he had just bruised a bone and it would heal by itself in a couple of weeks. I kept checking on him throughout the night and Tom said "I am okay mommy" but his leg was black and blue and swollen. The next morning, I stayed with Kelly at home and asked Randy to take Tom back to the doctor. Later that day Tom came home with the cast on his leg because it was broken. Another time he was riding along on the back of our neighbor kid's bicycle when he fell off and hit the back of his head on a rock that was sticking out from the street.

His head was bleeding heavily and I was alarmed, but his father was not around. I was panicking and wrapped his head with a towel and drove him to the hospital. While I was driving Tom was in the back seat crying from pain, and I started to cry with him. Suddenly Tom stopped crying and said "Mom I am not hurt, please don't cry, see I am not hurt, I am smiling" and cracked a little smile. Even as a grown man, he is always concerned about my well-being and often stopped by to check on me. Tom bought his first home when he was 25 years old. It was a brand-new house with an unfinished family room up above the tow car garage and unfinished landscape.

Tom got married in that house and him and his wife let me stay with them when I didn't have a place to go. His wife is beautiful, hard worker and there was time that they helped me with my car payments when I decided to get a place of my own until I married to Jake. Tom and his wife have one child and they moved up to NH where they have a good school system and a safe place to raise their child. Tom is a good provider for his family and an awesome dad to his son, and loves his wife. His wife came from foreign country just like me but she is well spoken, successful and loves her husband and their only child and I appreciate her so very much. Their boy, my grandson is a loving and handsome boy who has blonde hair and is extremely smart. He mastered the alphabet before he reached 2 years old and he reads at a 3rd grade level, even before he started the first grade. He loves music and the arts, both performing and visual arts and reads music well when he plays piano. I had the privilege to live with them for a while and watched him grow from infant to toddler and I enjoyed every moment. Nevertheless, all my grandchildren are very smart and I feel so blessed.

I remembered one incident when Tom was in high school. He was in track team at his school and also the church we were attending. He had an opportunity to compete at the University in Pennsylvania and he went with one of his friend's family. The next day I was on my way to P.A. to join them and it was my first long distance driving alone. No one had GPS back than and I used paper map like everyone else in those days. I was doing fine until when I got to the P.A. and with the busy traffic, I got lost and drove around few hours before I came up on the remote place with the sign in front of me says "detour". It was getting dark and I had no idea how to get around because there was no following sign that guide to get around the area. I thought, "maybe I can pass through somehow" and proceeded to drive. Now I am in the wooded area with no lights except the head lights from my car and I couldn't early see far head. Suddenly "clunk" and my car tilted to right side and got stuck. I hastily jump out from the car and saw that the passenger side of the tire was half way into the large hole. I shouted for help but off course there were no one was around. I shut the light off to avoid draining the battery and crawled to the backseat and lock the car doors. At early dawn I step out of the car and walked around to see where I was and I was in shock. Not even a quarter-miles ahead of where I got stuck, there was a cliff with water beneath the cliff!! Made the long story short, the place I got stuck was not too far from the university and I was rescued by Tom's friends and I brought him home safely.

My youngest son Kirk is a Hip-Hop artist, who writes and performs his own music. He has been into the music since he was 14 years old and I remember finding poems and lyrics everywhere in his room and now his music is marketed all the way to Japan. Kirk's music producer is Japanese and he is a wonderful, talented guy, and so is his beautiful wife. You see, even though there is bad history between Korea and Japan, person to person, we are the same human being and I appreciate them. Come what may, Kirk suffered from a terrible anxiety disorder but I believe music saved him. I remember he said that when he holds the microphone, even if he was on the stage with hundreds of people, all of his anxiety "just fades away" like a smoke into the sky. He is now married to the most beautiful, caring and amazing woman who is in fashion industry. She designs incredible fashion jewelry and she does her own marketing and now she has her own show room. Their wedding day was the most gorgeous day, with perfect weather and beautiful scenery and I am grateful to his mother in law who made the day so perfect. She also generously rented inns for my family to stay for the wedding day and we all enjoyed the beautiful white sandy beach the next day. With her help, Kirk also worked for a school with troubled teens and made differences in their lives.

Kirk's mother-in-law is a loving and kind woman who treats him like her own son. I can't say that I've always been a good mother. I was restricted with my kids at times, including spanking when I thought they needed discipline. One time when Kelly and Tom were 4 and 5, they brought to me what looked like a real diamond ring for me and said that they

found it in the trash can by the neighbor's
yard sale. I thought they just took it from
the yard sale and I spanked them and
took them to apologize to the owner. I felt
so bad when I found out that the owner
had in fact thrown the ring in the trash
because "it was just from Avon" This
memory still haunts me from time to time
for me being "ignorant". There are times
that I was too busy chasing dreams and
didn't fully pay attention to little things
when I think they needed me the most
and I am so sorry.

Looking back to my study years,
after getting my GED at age 52, I started
to study Liberal Arts at North Shore
Community College and It was my first
day of college. I was ever so proudly
carrying books and notebooks in my arms
as I walked down the hallway. From a
short distance I could see the professor
standing at the classroom door and
greeting each student as they entered the
classroom. He said "welcome to my class"
as the person before me entered. I was
smiling as I took one step closer when the

professor put out his hand and stopped me. He had a stern look on his face and said "you are in the wrong class the ESL class is down the hallway around the corridor" as he pointed down the hallway. I was upset at his ignorance for assuming all Asians were there to learn English as a second language. Enduring his class for the entire semester was not an easy task. He often humiliated me in front of the whole class, making fun of my writing. He would say things like "What? I don't even know what you are trying to say" and many students would giggle or laugh. There was more than one occasion that he made a joke out of my writing, which made me cry and be embarrassed. I finally tried to report him to the Assistant Dean of the school, but no follow up was made.

Regardless of the unpleasant experiences from my first class in college, I earned my Associate Degree to include the study of criminal justice. After receiving my Associates Degree, I applied for my Bachelor's degree in counseling at the school for Human Services at Lesley

University, and I got accepted. It took me literally 7 years to earn my B.S. because I had to maintain a full-time job while studying for my degree. However, even before I got my Bachelor's degree, I was scouted by the Program Director at a relapse prevention program at the same agency where I was working, with a substantial pay increase and my own desk, phone, computer and beeper, (yes, we proudly carried around beepers in those days). There was no more driving the community van, grocery shopping or cooking... not that I minded at all but I knew I was on my way in a career path in mental health field. A year later, I followed my mentor from Plowshares program to Danvers residential program at the same agency. From that program, she recommended me to apply for Shift Supervisor's position and I am sure with her good word, I got the job.

Several years later I was promoted to be the Program Director at a residential program in Newburyport at the same agency. The program was at an upscale facility and consisted of 4 male and 4 female residents with mental illness. There were rumors that I was promoted to the director position because the agency was facing a court case from a past employee involving racism. Maybe the rumor was true, because several months later I was transferred to another program. The reason they gave me was "we are restructuring the position requirements and you don't have college degree" and I was advised "we can transfer you to different program or you can quit, but it's up to you". Well, I took the position because I needed the job. The Danvers program was a small cottage with 4 male clients who spent most of their adult life in Danvers State Hospital. If you never heard of Danvers State Hospital, there is a movie called Session 9, which is about the facility, are Insane Asylum built in 1874.

When Danvers State Hospital closed
down because of its patient mistreatment,
the patients were sent to a variety of
places including small cottages situated
on lower ground of the hospital property.
When I took over the position, the
cottages were in chaos with stained
furniture, torn blinds on the windows,
holes in the walls and trash were all
around the house. In addition, all of the
staff disliked me because their new boss
was not just any woman, but also an
Asian woman. This was shared with me
by my assistant, who later became my
trusted confidant. I requested extra
money in the budget from the agency and
changed furniture. I bought cheap fabrics
and made beautiful curtains for every
window. The problem was most of staff
was used to sitting in front of the TV with
a remote control, and did the minimal
amount of work possible and were also
disrespectful to the clients. t took a lot of
effort, but I changed all of that, not with
force or arguments, but with me being an
example to all of the staff. We cleaned
trash around the cottage, planted flowers,

and decorated the inside with indoor plants and art work. I also requested maintenance to fix the big holes in the wall and replaced all the broken blinds on the windows. I did all this between my administrative work. When clients came home from the day treatment, they were amazed with the new atmosphere and said "Wow, this is our home?" and I replied "yes, it is your home". I remember one of the clients, I will call B. He was in his 50's but functioned as a child. He would take out pots, pans and canned goods from the cupboard, and lay them on the floor to play with. He would sit across the table in awe as he watched me sew curtains for the windows and smiled. When I took over the program, this client's only source of nutrition was Ensure, because he did not know how to feed himself. I hired a Korean woman who did an excellent job with him. We made some Korean dishes together and began to teach him how to feed himself. She would get a spoon full of tasty mixed rice and place it in his mouth and just leave it there. He soon realized he had food in his mouth, and he took out the spoon and started to chew and we repeated. He soon learned how to feed himself and enjoyed the Korean food.

As a Program Director, I oversaw all medications and finances and I was also what one would call a "Rep-Payee", which meant that I could assist the client with his finances. I noticed that he had accumulated a lot of money in his account, and with his sister's approval, who was his guardian, I purchased a big screen TV for his room. We also purchased a keyboard for him, which he enjoyed playing though he didn't read the music. We sometimes let the music play by itself and we would all dance to the music, and he loved to dance.

I also held weekly staff meetings with lunch and also paid the employees for attending meetings, and soon no one missed the meetings. We would discuss the schedule, job responsibilities, getting ready for annual licensing and training for treating clients with respect. The program became very organized, and staff were taking their job more seriously and we made our workplace a friendly environment. About 2 years later, our program was transferred to a larger, brand new facility in Beverly and I remained as the Program Director for 4 more years. I enjoyed my job and had formed a good working relationship with all of the staff; in fact, the man who disliked me the most at the beginning became my right-hand man and confidant.

Chapter Nine

At the beginning of my professional years, before I became the Program Director, I met Jake. He was working for Lucent Technology but also had his barber's license, and he had a little shop set up in the basement of his home as a side job. At the time, I was a shift supervisor at an Amesbury group facility with 8 clients through Health & Education Services. All of our clients had severe mental health issue and I oversaw client's medication management, financial status, and staff schedules and activities during my work hours. We had a barber who came to the residence to provide monthly haircuts for our clients, but she was on maternity leave and that was how I got to meet Jake. He was a friend of one of our staff members and he was introduced to me as an option to fill in for our other barber. Jake was charming, outgoing and made our clients feel safe and comfortable and I appreciated for his professionalism.

A month later, Jake invited me to see "Miss Saigon" at the North Shore Music Theater, which was our very first date. We met at the parking lot of a shopping center, and when I complimented that I liked his shirt he said "I got this at the Salvation Army store for $1.00." I laughed because I was wearing a sweater that I paid $1.00 at the Salvation Army thrift store. That thrift store was my favorite store in those days because there was no stress for high cost items and they had plenty of stuff to look around. It was one of my "self-care" strategies and self-therapy. I told Jake about the one unpleasant experience at the thrift store I had: I was going through the clothes rack and saw one shirt was on the floor. I tried to be nice and pick up the shirt to place over the rack. Suddenly, a middle age woman who appeared to be working there shouted "Can you put that shirt on hanger?!" than she added "people have no respect!" I told her that I didn't see an empty hanger and I also was not the one who dropped the shirt on the floor. She then turned around and said loudly "We should put the damn people back in the boat and send them back where they came from!!" I took that comment very personally and reported it to the store manager, but I don't think anything happened. The next trip to the store, I saw her working and she gave me a "dirty look" and mumbled something under her breath, but it didn't stop me shopping there. Jake was humorous and when he heard the story he said "Tell her you missed the boat, next time you see her".

I had seen Miss Saigon at Wang's theater before and the play left a lasting impression on me; I enjoyed it even more the second time around. Maybe it was because I understood the similarity of the story, where many Korean women in camp towns had to face the same challenges. If you have never seen the show, Miss Saigon, she was one of the prostitutes in a GI's village in Vietnam during the war. She was in love with one of the soldiers who unwillingly left her behind when troops were called back to the U.S. After her lover left Saigon, she found out that she was pregnant with his child. After giving birth to her son, she continued to work as prostitute, endlessly hoping for her child's father to return and find her. To make the long story short, the soldier did return to Saigon but only to claim his child because he was already married to an American woman in U.S. Miss Saigon was heartbroken with her undying love for him, at the same time she wanted her son to have the life she dreamed of with his father. Yet she couldn't bear the thought of living life without her son, so she shot herself and died. I sobbed again as Miss Saigon took her last breath.

Jake was outgoing, sweet and kind hearted. We met in November and he took me to Florida in February to meet his grandfather, and surprised me with a gold bangle bracelet with diamonds inlaid all the way around for Valentine's day. We also took a trip to a place called Captiva Island, where only the richest few with private jets lived. There were no automobiles allowed, and every household had golf carts to get around. The island had absolutely breath-taking views with white powder like sandy beaches and crystal-clear blue water. The night sky seemed so close to the earth with the millions of stars. The stars felt as though you could almost open your hand and swipe a handful of them. Jake was not a rich man, but his sister in law's mother (brother's wife) owned the place there and we stayed with them for three days. Nonetheless, Jake had his own demons. He was a recovering alcoholic and AA was in his life, also he loved women. He admitted that womanizing was in his nature and he couldn't help himself, because it's in his blood. I also learned that Jake was given up for adoption right from the hospital in NY when he was only 4 days old. He was adopted by a loving couple from Andover, MA. and he grew up with 3 other siblings who were biological children to his adopted parents. Although his adopted family was loving people, Jake had a troubled childhood and adulthood, and his story saddened my heart. He had many affairs during our relationship but he came up with an excuse each time, and

I forgave him over and again; besides I thought, he was 17 years younger than I was. Eventually enough was enough and I ended the relationship, but he continued to contact me for reconciliation, but I refused.

Three months after we broke up, I got a phone call from Lawrence General Hospital stating that Jake was stabbed was in critical condition, and I was his emergency contact. When I got to the hospital he was in surgery, which took 6 hours. The nurse handed me a bag containing his bloody shirt, pants, cut up belt and blood-stained pair of shoes. It was irony that the belt and shoes were the same thing he wore when I first met him. Later, I learned that Jake was stabbed by a young guy with a 9-inch blade, cutting part of his lung, liver and the stomach. Jake was already without a spleen from a past injury. After I regrouped myself, I contacted his family to inform them of the incident. His adopted parents were divorced early on; his father and younger brother were living in California his sister was living in Connecticut and his mother was in Andover. His entire family, except his oldest brother came to the hospital and stayed in the area for a while. Jake had to go for 2 more surgeries because fluid kept building up in his lung.

The hospital also put Jake on morphine which caused side effects, and he was acting out of control. He would get up from the bed, try to clean bloody sheets, throw bed pans and try to put on t-shirts through his leg, and more. When the nurse came, she would struggle to put him back in the bed and during struggle, he hit the treating nurse by accident. The hospital security was called in and they called police and Jake was arrested. Police didn't notice that he had just had an operation and he still had drainage bags attached from his rib cage into the machine, which got detached during the struggle. Inside the elevator, police beat him up with batons, leaving cuts and bruises on his face, arms and ankles. I wasn't there when this happened, but I was horrified to learn that hospital didn't do anything to help him. That evening I got a call from Jake on his way to Bridgewater State Hospital and I wailed. He said that one of the kind guards let him use his cell phone to make the call and he was letting me know what was going on. He said that he was in lot of pain; he was scared and I felt helpless. I didn't understand why he had deep wounds that were still bleeding and they were sending him to the psychiatric jail. However, when he got to Bridgewater, the hospital refused to accept him because of his medical condition. Jake was sent back to the Lawrence General Hospital and placed on the 4th floor, hand cuffed to the bed. Later he got transferred to the Whidden Memorial Hospital in Everett MA., where he remained for a month. Since Jake had addictive symptoms/personality they could not put him on any type of pain killer, and put him on methadone instead. Jake continued to seek my help and I didn't have the heart to turn him away. I took one semester off from my studies and promised myself that I would help him only until he got well enough to take care of himself.

After he got discharged from the hospital Jake flushed the rest of the methadone he was given into the toilet and he began having withdrawal symptoms at home. He refused to go to the hospital because he knew that they would just put him back on the methadone again. For several days he was in bed shivering with cold sweats, vomiting, and having convulsions, and it was painful to watch him suffer. I sat by him day and night and tried to take care of him. My youngest son Kirk, who was in his early 20's at the time, was living with me, but my apartment was not far from Jake's home. I was going back and forth to make sure Kirk had the things he needed and after 4-5 nights of the terrible ordeal with Jake he was well enough to sit up and swallow some liquid without puking. It took him months before he could get up and walk again because of the damage done to his organs.

Before the incident, Jake had his own barber shop in downtown Haverhill and did well with his business. He left the Lucent Tech job when the company office in North Andover closed down and pursued opening his own barber business. When he got well and returned to his work, he wanted go for a ride to NH. We stopped in front of a jewelry store and decided to go in. The store owner brought out precious looking princess cut diamond rings and Jake proposed to me; I was overjoyed.

Less than one year after Jake proposed, we got married at Castleton in Windham, NH and Jake paid for the entire cost of the wedding, including my wedding dress and his own ring. The weather was gorgeous, the place was beautiful, and the guests were gathered. My wedding dress was what I had always dreamed of, with a beautiful tiara. The princess like dress was elegant off white, bare shoulders with a thin stripe tide back and wide spread out buttons that reached the ground. My daughter was my maid of honor, my daughter in law and my granddaughter were the bridesmaids and my son Tom gave me away.

My son Kirk moved in with us when my apartment lease was over and Jake was good to him. Kirk was with us for a few years, sometimes without a job, but Jake never once complained and I appreciated him for it. Kirk was working on his music and eventually he got a job and also a girlfriend whom he is married to now and moved out on his own. I resumed my studies, took evenings and weekend classes, and had many sleepless nights while doing this and maintaining a full-time job. After the completion of my B.S. in Human Services at Lesley, I pursued a Master's Degree in Express Therapy with Psychology at the same university. Expressive therapy is unlike traditional talk therapy; it is an art expression, and the process of creation is emphasized rather than the final product. Expressive therapy is predicated on the assumption that people can heal through use of the imagination, and other various forms of creative expression. This includes practice of using imagery, story-telling, dance, music, drama, poetry, movement, and visual arts, together in an integrated way to foster human growth, development and promote healing. It is about reclaiming our innate capacity as human beings for creative expression of our individual and collective human experience in artistic form.

Have I achieved successfully an understanding of all forms of expressive therapy? Absolutely not, but I have gained extensive knowledge and experiences to apply to my work. Sometimes without realizing it, I use them daily with adult clients, even when I am just exercising with them. When my current job was in a different facility years ago, I worked for the program as an intern as part of my pursuit for my

Master's degree. The one fine memory I have, on top of leading meditation and art groups and being an assistant to their Mindfulness trial-based therapy, is that I created a 'Fashion show' for the clients. I chose 10 clients who were shy, timid and had a lack of self-confidence. There was one particular client who always wore long sleeved turtlenecks, even in the hot weather. Her hair would literally cover her face and she was always looking down. I worked tirelessly with these clients, and on the day of the show, she was transformed to a beautiful woman with confidence, and she even shook her hips in front of the fashion show judges (who were also clients). The show was truly a success, people often talk about it, even after years have passed.

For all that, I graduated in December 2011 with my Master's Degree, all while continuing to work a full-time job in the mental health field. On May 20, 2012, I walked the stage to receive my diploma while my children watched in anticipation. I was 64 years old, and the oldest woman to receive a diploma for her Master's degree on that stage. The following year, I begin to pursue my Doctorate for Clinical Psychology through online classes, but it was just too overwhelming for me. I am a visual learner and need to be in the classroom with others, watch the performance and listen to lectures. Instead I actually studied Theology at the Harvard extension school for one semester, but could not continue due to the financial matter. On top of financial burden, the theology course they taught was not what I had expected.

After 6 years of marriage with Jake, I found out that he was having an affair with a 29-year-old woman for quite some time, and that he also gambled away a lot of his earnings. When I found this out and confronted him, his response was "It is what it is". I was upset with him at the time, but I don't hold a grudge and I do not hate him... rather I feel sad for him. I also understand that I spent lot of hours on evenings and weekends to study and attend the classes and I have much to blame for his infidelity. Three years after we separated, we officially ended the marriage in 2016.

Jake was never a bad person, he was generous and had a good heart. He was also a victim of his mother who abandoned him, regardless of the reason, and this is not a judgement but honest fact. I often thought about my two sons in Korea and wondered how they were doing. When the night is quite and Jake is at sound sleeping, I felt sorrow for him and my two children I left behind. Jake did find his birth mother, along with her other children when he was about 44 years old. Jake is loyal to his friends, AA buddies, both sides of his family and always generous. I remember the day he surprised me with the most beautiful car that I loved driving. One morning I got ready for work, grabbed the key for my Toyota and walked out the front door, where I saw a black Lexus sports car across the street. I thought to myself "Damn, somebody has a really nice car" as

I tried opening the door of my Toyota with the manual roll down window. For some reason my key didn't fit and then I thought it looked like I may have grabbed Jake's car keys by accident, which was for his Lexus sedan. I went back to the house and hurried upstairs "Honey where is my car key?". Jake, still in bed half sleeping replied "I hope you like your new car" I said "What? Do you mean that black car is mine?" and he said "Yes honey go and enjoy your ride!" "Wow, wow, I can believe what just happened" I exclaimed as I hurried out the door.

On my way to work with the hard-top down, I really felt like a rich woman. It had a plush dark brown leather seats, and was a two-door sports car with the automatic hard top, that I only needed to push a button for the top to go down into the trunk. Jake often placed $100.00 bills inside the cover of built-in GPS for extra spending money. I tried to keep the good memories of him alive and let the bad ones slip away. Anyhow, I totaled that beautiful car by hitting some trees on a snowy day trying avoid the car which was following too close behind me. luckily, I only had concussion. Within one year after the separation I totaled another brand-new car, less than one year after totaling my Lexus. People often joke with me, saying that I have "nine lives". By the way, Jake and I maintain a good friendship. His girlfriend left him after they stayed together for 3 years. Now a days, Jake often invites me to dinner, a movie or a comedy show, but does not expect anything in return. People said "stay away from him, he is a trouble maker". Can people change? That is the million-dollar question, because nobody knows the real answer. I feel comfortable staying as his friend than as a wife and we both enjoy time spent together without any expectations. I hope he find the person he is looking for and be at peace and happy with himself.

Chapter Ten

It has been 43 years since the giant silver wings carried me and my daughter Kelly over the Pacific Ocean. I will be celebrating my 71st birthday in this coming November which is next month with my wonderful and loving family. I work as an individual therapist at an outpatient clinic, work with troubled children, and handle some with DCF (Department of Children and Family) cases with their family as an In-Home Therapist. I treated each child and family with compassion and integrity. However, I suffered heart attack in Dec. 2017 and had a cardiac catheterization with stents placed, I cut down my work to 24 hours. I continue to work for Adult Behavioral Learning Center at Lahey Health Behavioral Services. My cardiologist informed that my heart problem was most likely hereditary, but stress can add more risk for having another heart attack.

The Lahey Health Behavioral Services was merged with our old agency, North East Behavioral Services, previously known as Health and Education Services and now we are also a part of the Beth Israel Hospital system. I have the most amazing boss and friendly co-workers, including an office manager we call Rosy who is sweet, caring and always brings food for all staff. In fact, her lovely daughter was the one who offered me to edit my book and I am so grateful for both of them. Since I cut down my work hours, I created groups for the clients including dance exercise, chair yoga and dumbbell exercise, and Indoor walking exercise. The combination of mind and body groups to boost emotional and physical health have been successful, and I am having lots of fun with them. The behavioral learning center consists of 40-50 clients who are mentally challenged and/or duel diagnosed with the substance abuse individuals. They learn through DBT (dialectical behavioral therapy), CBT (cognitive behavioral therapy) and the Mindfulness-based therapy, in addition to recovery groups. The music therapy is very popular in our program and clients also have the opportunity to be involved in cooking, writing, arts and crafts and other varieties of groups. We recently started a drama group, which is run by a peer leader, as well as Tai Chi group and students take a great pride for doing all.

Since I cut down my hours, my job responsibilities have also changed to best fit my hours of work. I am now responsible for the intake of new clients that involve diagnostic evaluations. I am also responsible for new and updated treatment plans for all clients and the requesting treatment authorizations from health insurance companies, which keeps me pretty busy. I still run the exercise class because I love working out with the clients to encourage healthy living.

My mother died of cardiac arrest at age 74 and my father passed away after having a massive stroke at age 75, but until their passing I sent money whenever my mother needed. I didn't get to either of

their funeral services, nor my younger
sisters, who died at age 31. She was
murdered by her husband, and left behind
her beloved one-year old son. My loving
brother-in-law (husband of my older
sister) passed away in his sleep at age 65,
and after that I lost contact with all my
family in Korea. About 10 years ago, I
visited Korea with a non-profit women's
charity organization. We were there to
visit elders who spent their life in the U.S.
military villages servicing GIs which they
call "yankee whore" or "western whore".
These women were suffering a terrible
ordeal without medical care and
affordable housing. The Korean
government refused to admit their
involvement in sex slavery for decades.

They tried to hide the fact that the
Korean government allowed sex slavery
operations with human trafficking in
order to bring American dollars to Korea.
I know this is a "fact" because I was there
and witnesses and experienced through
all. In present day, there is a movement
for women's right in South Korea. "More

than 120 prostitutes who worked near U.S. military base are seeking compensation from country's government after it actively facilitated their work" (Daily News in Korea). Among those women now they are in their 70's, 4 of them were accompanied by staff from Korea to speak at women's organization conventions in St. Louis in 2015. Our organization paid the cost for their airfare and lodging to the convention while I was serving as president for the Boston Massachusetts region.

The reason it took this long for me to write my story was the fear of sacrificing my children's welfare. If my story ever got to be published, they may have to deal with the stigmatism and judgement from others because of my true identity from the past. Would they be embarrassed for the path that I have traveled? Would they be ashamed of me as their mother or be resentful for me afflicting emotional disturbance on them? I am still torn by this wondering "should I keep silence till day I die?" or "claim the power of my voice" and be an instrument for others, a voice for those who continue to suffer from ignorance of others. Nevertheless, I was one of the lucky ones to be set free from the mental and physical degradation, and I feel that I owe it to those women who died and were buried in an abandoned field. I owe it to women who have been kept in silence, marginalized by government, murdered and be forgotten.

I will be 71 years old in another month and live in apartment in NH, where I can be closer to my two older kids, their spouses, 3 grand-children and one great-granddaughter. My youngest one and his wife lives south of Boston and I get to see them time to time, though not as often as I would like to. My younger grandson from Tom has blond hair and my great-granddaughter has blue eyes; they are so precious and beautiful. I am certain that my later generations would not recognize that they had full blood Korean ancestors. One of my old acquaintances once mocked me for ending up in one-bedroom apartment alone in old age. She was right, I have never owned a house, and no man ever truly understood me enough to stand by me, but I am content with myself for being who I am today. I also realized that I am a damaged woman and I have the tendency to sabotage relationships in fear of abandonment, but that is a story for another time. I am still working and earn my own living because I want to take care of myself as long as I am able. Honestly, I tried the low-income apartment recently, but I was denied because I make "a little too much money". But if I quit my job, I don't make enough money to survive, so I am stuck in between a rock and a hard place, but I am okay with that. There are a lot of others who are worse off than I am. It also saddens me to say that there is an unseen parallel even among inter-culturally married Korean women. Some are quick to say "I did not meet my husband in camp town" "My husband was civilian when we met" "I was a professional when I met my husband" "I've never lived in camp town". What they are really saying is "I am not the same as you are, yankee whore". Most of them who profess them self as "clean" are so call "Christians" and they try their best to separate them-selves from woman like me. I would like to ask them, does this means you are better than I? "Does your God believe that you are better than me?" In what way??

Come what may, I am more confident with myself than ever before, and I am finally at my peace and cautiously happy being alone. I talk and text with my kids often and try to see them whenever we have a chance. I also see them on Facebook, and I download photos of my grandkids for keepsakes. My place is clean, charming, comfortable, and I have everything I need. I hear birds chirping, little chipmunks and wild rabbits visit my patio for breadcrumbs from time to time. I see red robins hopping from one bush to another and even humming birds trying to get nectar out of the cascading reddish pink flowers from my hanging basket by the patio door. The red maple tree with dark red leaves dances in the summer breeze and

the sun rays the part of my living room. I
hear a puppy barking from the distance....
When the time comes and I am unable to
work, I will settle down in elderly housing
but that is just my own plan because I will
never know what tomorrow will bring.

As I was finishing up my writing,
our family had most beautiful gathering
to celebrate my granddaughter's
wedding. The venue for wedding
ceremony was held in lakeside views with
beautiful scenery with the waterfall at the
entrance. My daughter and her husband
did a fine job preparing the wedding for
their daughter and her husband and I was
ever so proud of them. The outdoor
ceremony by the lakeside as the sun lays
low and the mixture of dyes serenely
beams the water and over the horizon.
Astoundingly beautiful bride,
bridesmaids and the handsome groom
with his brother as the best man, the
groom's man which was my older
grandson... Alongside the two little
handsome ring bearers, my grandson
from Tom and the bride's little cousin and

a pretty flower girl who is groom's first daughter... and adorable baby girl my great granddaughter.... the music, food, speech and the loving guests. All my children, grandchildren and extended family and friends all gathered. My great granddaughter sound sleep in my arms as I gaze at the dance floor, watching her half-sister, my grandson and other kids dancing. It truly made me felt like I am in the mists of one loving family. I believe it was because there was so much love in the room. I set by my daughter's in-laws as we shared an old memory of when our children were young. We both agreed that how fortunate and blessed we are as growing into an old age with each other. My ever-growing family is a "multiracial" and I am proud of each and every ethnicity we share as one family. We are mixed with an Italian, German, English, Irish, Native American, Brazilian, Portuguese, Lebanon, Greek, French Canadian, of course Korean and we are peaceful family with love and respect for one another.

In all fairness, I must say that the unfortunate circumstances have favored me with spiritual and emotional growth. The growth that I can share with others to encourage and inspire that there is a "Silver lining behind every cloud" if you don't give up. I learn to endure woeful circumstances with perseverance and dedication in the face of adversity. America..... the land of freedom and this is my home. I believe that this is the greatest country on earth, if you learn to appreciate what the country stands for, take responsibility and do your part as citizen. The freedom did not come free but bought by the blood and sweats of pioneers and the people who perished to saved the land. I have lived in this country longer than where I was born and raised. My ash will be spread in this soil. My legacy will sustain through my children, their children and the generations to come.

I asked my kids to cremate me when I die. I don't need a wake, funeral, expensive coffin or a fancy tombstone. I have faith in my God, the Yahuwah who has the power to gather me from the dust if he is willing. He will resurrect me from the dust to meet my Messiah the Yahushua at the second resurrection. I pray that my children and their family will gain the knowledge of the true gospel and receive everlasting life in the new Kingdom of heaven on earth. Until then, my spirit will rest in peace.

I often passes by the Robert Frost farm on my way to work and back in Derry NH where I reside. His old farm is located on Rt. 28 about five minutes from my apartment complex. It was the home of Frost and his family from 1900-1911, one of the nation's most acclaimed poets. Who knew I would be living near his farm house, the poet I admired the most when I was in Korea. Life is certainly a strange one.

Still and all, the ill-fated childhood plagued me with the silent cries but I rebuilt my shattered life with the grace of God and I am the pioneer of my own legacy. I am blessed with my ever-growing family and I love them so dearly.... If there is a wish or even a bucket list, I want to travel to Korea and visit my ancestors grave to pay tribute and attend the annual ceremony of them. I am certain that the chromosomes I inherited from my ancestors, yield the consistent thread through the generations and bestowed upon me with the force to be who I am today. I will end my story with one of my favorite Poem by Robert Frost "I took the one less traveled by, And that has made all the difference."

Thank you for reading and please, accept my unending gratitude.

Un Chu Lee-Hoyle

Made in the USA
Las Vegas, NV
15 May 2021

23109153R00163